Praise for Dr. Lee Jampolsky and his work:

"The reader witnesses an actual process of healing as it unfolds. ...g , recommended."

—Library Journal

"Dr. Jampolsky's . . . practical spirituality is both inspiring and transforming. His compassionate approach to life is an antidote to our stressful times."

—Marianne Williamson, author of A Return to Love

". . . Lee Jampolsky will bring light to your world and could change it forever . . . with profound wisdom, Lee opens the way. . ."

—Neale Donald Walsch, author of Conversations with God

"A miracle of truthful discovery, one that inspires as it heals."

—Jean Houston, Ph.D., author of The Possible Human

". . . contains a deep understanding of the problem and a thoroughly com passionate set of solutions . . . balanced and effective."

—Hugh Prather, author of Notes to Myself

"Be encouraged, inspired, and helped by the examples and insights."

—Jean Shinoda Bolen, M.D., author of Ring of Power

"For every man or woman who has ever struggled."

—John Gray, Ph.D., author of Men Are from Mars, Women Are from Venus

"Guides people through the daily stresses of life with hope and optimism."

—Caroline Myss, author of Why People Don't Heal and How They Can

"Helps to find greater understanding, healing, forgiveness, and love."

—Michael Murphy, author of Golf in the Kingdom

"Jampolsky gives me confidence that we all have access to everything we need to know to live our lives well."

—Hal Zina Bennett, author of The Lens of Perception

Healing the Addictive Personality

*Freeing Yourself
from Addictive Patterns
and Relationships*

Dr. Lee Jampolsky

CELESTIAL ARTS
Berkeley

Celestial Arts and the Celestial Arts colophon are registered trademarks of Random House, Inc..

Cover and text design by Katy Brown
Production by Colleen Cain

Library of Congress Cataloging-in-Publication Data

Jampolsky, Lee L., 1957–
Healing the addictive personality : freeing yourself from addictive patterns and relationships / Lee Jampolsky.
p. cm.
Includes bibliographical references and index.
ISBN 1-58761-315-8 (978-1-58761-315-9 : alk. paper)
1. Compulsive behavior. 2. Addicts—Rehabilitation. I. Title.

RC533.J37 2008
616.85′84—dc22

2007014557

Printed in the United States of America

11 10 9 8 7 6 5 4

For Jalena and Lexi,
in gratitude for the most precious journey of my life

CONTENTS

4 The Structure
of the Truth–Based Personality

5 The Thirteen Core Beliefs
of the Truth–Based Personality

6 The Addictive Personality and the Fear of Intimacy 103

7 Learning to Recognize Our Essential Value 119

INTRODUCTION

Running from my pain had become as normal as relieving an itch by scratching. For much of my life I had been fighting feelings of low self-esteem, and it had become easier for me to condemn myself than it was to see beyond the many mistakes I kept repeating over and over again. I longed for the emptiness within me to be filled, at the same moment never believing it could be filled. For years I settled for the fleeting, fragmented moments of relief that my many addictions seemed to offer. I thought that the next accomplishment, relationship, drug, or dollar would bring me the contentment I craved.

For nearly three decades much of my personal and professional life has been devoted to understanding and healing addiction. In the process I have learned about happiness and what allows us to grow from our challenges. It is this journey that I share with you. I offer not a panacea to addiction but rather a means to better know and accept yourself. It is my belief that where there is acceptance, there is no need for addiction, and happiness is discovered.

In this book, addiction is perhaps defined in a broader sense than you may be accustomed to. I address the Addictive Personality as part of a human condition that affects many, if not most, people. If, like me, you have ever felt that your happiness was dependent on someone else's behavior, getting some new possession or more money, being in a certain place, having sex, or a specific outcome to a situation, this book is addressed to you. When you see the phrase "Addictive Personality" in this book, you may mentally replace it with the phrase, "the part of my mind that pursues happiness in things (people, places, substances) external to myself."

If you are tired of hiding from the world, can't run any faster on the treadmill, or realize that more does not equal happier, I suggest that you resist the temptation to decide whether you do or don't have an Addictive

Personality. Instead, approach the material in a self-reflective way, asking, "On a scale of one to ten, how much does this describe me?" The extent to which we are stuck in our addictive patterns caused by the Addictive Personality is the extent to which we inhibit our potential for happiness and new opportunities. This book can open your life to happiness and opportunity, but it also may challenge you. I invite you to approach it without the need to immediately believe what is set forth. Although some of it may seem foreign, with an open mind try practicing the principles and pay attention to what results.

You would not likely be reading this book if your life was going just how you want it. No doubt you have made attempts at positive change without the results you desired. The ideas presented in this book are straightforward and practical but, because of old patterns of thinking and behaving, these new ideas can be easily forgotten or denied. For this reason I repeat the central themes in many different ways. This may seem redundant to some, but I think the repetition may be useful for others.

Many of the central ideas presented in this book are a continuation of my earlier book *Healing the Addictive Mind*, which, in part, utilized the principles of *A Course in Miracles*. Certain concepts and titles paraphrase that material. The information and descriptions in the vignettes about my clients have been altered in order to ensure confidentiality. With the exception of stories about myself, or where a last name is given, all names, identifying information, and other factors have been changed. Any resemblance that you may find between the vignette and somebody that you know is purely coincidental.

—Dr. Lee Jampolsky

The Path to Happiness and the Road to Misery Are Easily Confused

If I asked you if you wanted to be totally happy or completely miserable, pretty much everyone gives the same answer. Yet, because of the Addictive Personality, we seem to constantly come up short in the happiness department.

It is safe to say that you didn't wake up one morning and set out to become as miserable as possible. Dissatisfaction, hopelessness, frustration, and depression seem to sneak into a person's life through the back door. Most of us would not call ourselves addicts or choose to have addictive personalities, yet it is my observation that addictive personalities and the resulting addictive lifestyles are prevalent in our society. When we fail to recognize our Addictive Personality and how it becomes an addictive lifestyle void of true happiness, we continue to dig a deeper hole that becomes increasingly difficult to climb out of. Though we are not sure how it happened, we are not happy, so we seek to escape through endless pursuits for happiness outside ourselves. These pursuits have many faces and take many forms, ranging from acquiring more possessions or losing more weight to finding the right mate or making more money. These things in themselves are not necessarily bad, but for the Addictive Personality the pursuit becomes compulsive, endless, and all encompassing. No amount of success at getting what we think will make us happy is ever enough, so we remain miserable. It is time to stop running away and look more closely at just what an Addictive Personality and addictive lifestyle are. The good news is that you can heal both and discover true happiness.

Recognizing an Addictive Personality and the Purpose of Healing

In defining an Addictive Personality and addictive lifestyle, it is most important to look at the beliefs behind the behaviors. Only looking at behavior can be misleading, whereas finding the beliefs that lead to dissatisfaction and perpetuating the Addictive Personality can help us heal. It is also essential to define the purpose in our work of healing; otherwise the approach becomes one of "fixing the problem" rather than "growing from the process." Fixing the problem is always about surface change that doesn't necessarily make us better human beings. Growing from the process is about deepening our capacity to recognize opportunity and experience happiness. First, let's identify how the Addictive Personality evolves.

> An Addictive Personality is created when we believe that looking outside of ourselves for happiness will bring us what we want and need.

In contrast, healing begins when we recognize this process and begin to reverse it. It was the great anthropologist Gregory Bateson who first suggested that an addict is a person who has a deeper thirst. Speaking for myself, I believe I was very fortunate to have discovered my Addictive Personality because beneath it I found I was thirsty for purpose and meaning in my life, and the answer to my healing was in addressing this thirst. Although my healing took place over a long time, there were a few key transitions.

Close to thirty years ago I had relapsed in my substance use and had been using narcotics for about three months. One night, I found myself alone because, being an addict, I had pushed everyone in my life away. I began to cry uncontrollably. The sounds that escaped my mouth seemed ancient, primal, as though they had lain chained in the darkness of isolation within me for centuries. I struggled to speak through my tears to the abyss that was around and within me, as if the familiarity of my own voice would pull me out of the pain that enveloped me. But words would not come, and only the despair of deep loneliness filled me as I sobbed in that cold and lonely room. Then, for just a moment, I emerged from the depth of my pain, as if gasping for air in a sea of unknown depth.

I had been addicted to one thing or another for years. Prior to my relapse I had not used any mind-altering substance for an entire year. Back then I did not know about rehabilitation or recovery programs, and although I had been able to stop using drugs for periods of time, I had not really looked at what fueled my addictions. All I knew then was that all my life, no matter what I did, I felt that there was something missing. Prior to my relapse I remember thinking, "I don't take drugs anymore, and I'm still not happy. In fact, I am more depressed than ever. What's the use?"

Over the years I came to find that what was missing was the awareness and experience of love. What kept me from love was my constant pursuit of happiness in things external to myself, which, in turn, covered up my deep feelings of emptiness and aloneness. It was not until the crying episode that I even knew that I felt alone and separate from everybody and everything. Drugs and other distractions had been a dam holding back the floodwaters of my self-imposed exile from love. That night I came face to face with my worst fear: my aloneness.

I believed I was alone and isolated in a cruel and punishing world. So, I set out to fill the void by looking outside myself for things that I mistakenly thought would make me feel whole and that I belonged. But on that night, I realized that drugs, money, and relationships would not fill the emptiness within me. Only by removing the blocks to love that were created by my Addictive Personality could I begin to heal myself and find a sense of wholeness.

Today, I have come to see that overcoming my Addictive Personality has little to do with how tough I am on myself, or how much I try to control my life and addictions with sheer willpower. I tried these strategies for years and only ended up feeling more like a failure.

Looking back, I can see facets of my Addictive Personality driving my addictive search for satisfaction and gratification in things external to myself. I believe this to be true for each of us as individuals and, to some degree, on a societal level. Yet the existence of the Addictive Personality is somewhat controversial. This is because many of us look at people with addictions as weak and/or morally inferior, and we certainly don't want to see ourselves as members of this club! But if we consider Bateson's idea that the addict (a person with an Addictive Personality) is someone with a deeper thirst, it is harder to judge him or her (or ourselves) so harshly. Most people with addictive personalities, at one time or another, try to use food, alcohol, drugs, or other compulsive behaviors to momentarily slake this thirst. Of course, the result is more confusion and delusion. Addictive behaviors keep us disconnected from the feeling that there must be something more. When I finally stopped and recognized this longing in myself, I felt inspired to write the following poem.

THE QUIET PLACE INSIDE

The tangled roots of addiction
begin in my mind
when I believe that the world is
a land of trinkets promising happiness.

In this world I feel trapped,
surrounded by a moat of deep and shadowy
waters of loneliness and despair.
The knurled, spiny roots of addiction encase and
squeeze my heart, forcing the
memory of love to fade into darkness.

Let me today come to realize
that there is a quiet place inside of me,
a place kept safe for me,
where love lies protected and unharmed.

Today my awareness of love shines light
through the darkness of addiction.
The light of love is who I am.
Today I will take time to be still
and listen to the truth about who I am.

Healing Begins with the Invitation to Love

When we have an unhealed Addictive Personality we are often very lonely people. Even if we are with other people, or pursuing a goal, deep inside we are profoundly lonely. Sometimes we are completely unaware of this loneliness and don't realize all the suffering our failed attempts to relieve it creates. I know this very well from personal experience, as most of the first half of my life was spent either feeling very much alone or trying to run from that feeling. During moments of relative sobriety I can remember feeling that something was missing deep within me, like a constant ache I couldn't relieve. Fortunately, on that long-ago night of tears I discovered that, if properly perceived, this deep longing can be the beginning of healing because the "cure" for our aloneness is love.

I am not speaking of the kind of love the Addictive Personality sends us blindly seeking. The addict seeks to receive external love or tries to give an immature love that is based upon certain conditions being met. What I am speaking of is the experience of the unconditional love and compassion that is within our heart, and is available each and every moment.

Before I continue, I want to say that if I had read the above paragraph when I was in thrall to my Addictive Personality I would have immediately dismissed it as a bunch of psychobabble. At this point, some of what I am presenting may sound like empty "New Age" promises, or a naïve way of seeing the world, or just plain impossible considering your life. Yet, if you choose to read on, and undertake the daily lessons at the end of this book, you will know through your own experience exactly what I am speaking of.

The Four A's: Achieving, Acquiring, Approval, and Accomplishing

If the yearning for unconditional love and compassion goes unnoticed, our aloneness and the Addictive Personality continually feed off one another, perpetuating the pattern of addiction. I call this pattern of addiction the addictive lifestyle, and it is marked by a constant quest for the Four A's: Achieving, Acquiring, Approval, and Accomplishing. I know intimately well the effects of the Four A's. I wasted years of my life believing that if I could acquire something new, get approval from others, achieve a certain status in life, or accomplish some goal, I would find happiness. Despite the promises that the next possession, goal, situation, or person would fill the hole within me, the more I lived out a life ruled by the Four A's, the more alone and empty I felt. I tried to push away these uncomfortable feelings with more addictive behavior, which only escalated my dead-end search to a desperate frenzy. The result of the unhealed Addictive Personality is to be in the throes of an addictive lifestyle that is unrelenting, unending, and empty of true peace and happiness.

When the Solution Becomes Another Addiction

The solution is simple enough: To heal the Addictive Personality one must first recognize the Four A's and perceive the value of healing. However, there are obstacles. Many of us with Addictive Personalities have shied away from both emotional healing as well as any intellectual approach that might bring the Addictive Personality under scrutiny. Sometimes, when we attempt to do something positive, it may be unconsciously done so as not to heal the Addictive Personality, but continue it. Dealing with the Addictive Personality can be tricky because a new way of thinking can result in a blindly compulsive search for answers outside of ourselves. Be it in a church, therapist's office, college classroom, capital building, temple, or AA meeting, this kind of addictive search for answers is very common because virtually anything can become an addiction, including, paradoxically, what we think is our path out of addiction. Some of the markers of an addiction to a "solution" include: over-adhering to rules and dogma; becoming rigid, self-righteous, and intolerant toward other points of view; being incapable of doubting or questioning because every situation must be black or white, good or bad, right or wrong; being overwhelmed by shame and guilt, which continue to rule inner feelings and dictate outward behavior; adopting an overly simplistic attitude that problems can be "fixed" without much effort; believing that the chosen path is the only correct one and that those who don't follow it are wrong.

The way beyond an addictive solution is to first define the purpose of our undertaking. I define the healing of the Addictive Personality and addictive lifestyle as the process of awakening to love and compassion. Simply put, this is accomplished by removing the blocks to the awareness of love, which is the overall goal of this book. There is no singular right way to do this. Stated in as brief and direct way possible, opening our heart to love and truth in the present moment is the highest human experience, and is what healing the Addictive Personality is about.

Where to Find the Answers and How to Recognize the Smoke and Mirrors

Throughout the process of healing the Addictive Personality I will repeat the most important idea in a variety of ways because it takes time to fully embrace it, and you will be well served to remind yourself of it often.

When we look to anything other than our own minds for happiness, we are not going to find lasting peace or success.

Nearly all of us play the "If . . . then . . ." game: "If I get more money, then I will be happier." "If I get so-and-so to behave, then I will feel secure and loved." "If I get high, then I will not be so angry." "If I get approval from my boss, then I will know I am worthy." The list of the Addictive Personality's "If . . . thens" is endless. But we can't hide behind our addictive patterns and lifestyle and experience true happiness and wisdom no matter that our culture tells us quite the opposite. Being blind to the Addictive Personality and the resulting lifestyle has become the cultural norm today.

The answer to moving beyond this insanity is actually quite simple: Ask yourself, how would my awareness of myself and the world change this instant if I simply put all of my energy into welcoming love into my life and extending compassion to others? This is a very important question, for within it is the key to healing the Addictive Personality. Healing involves a disciplined effort to move beyond our external search for happiness and allow love to fill our heart. Healing involves ending the reign of harsh judgment on ourselves and others, and instead recognizing that a cocoon of kindness and gentility can envelop us. I have witnessed many tear-stained faces give birth to gentle, barely visible smiles as this happened. The moment we recognize love, the seeds of healing have been planted. Our feelings of aloneness don't altogether vanish, but our perception of it changes and certainly what we do with it changes. I have come to realize that the depth of my aloneness was shallow in comparison to the boundless depth of love. "Learning to love yourself is the definition of change." (Hugh Prather)

Biological Factors and Addiction

Because many people may have opinions as to whether chemical dependency and other addictions are a disease, or are interested in biological factors in general, it is important to briefly address this area. When I wrote *Healing the Addictive Mind*, more than fifteen years ago, there was increasing controversy as to what constitutes a disease, and if addiction was one. The debate has somewhat subsided as we appear closer to identifying a genetic predisposition to many diseases. I am of the opinion, as are many in the field, that in the future there will be a gene identified that plays a key role in addiction, and perhaps contributes to an Addictive Personality. However, I do not lose sight of the fact that this really would not change the need to understand and heal the emotional, cognitive, and spiritual aspects of addiction. Thus, it is my purpose to provide a broader perspective as to the origin, progression, and healing from all addictive behaviors and lifestyles.

When it comes to the subject matter of this book, I look at the word *disease* and see a word that describes the present state of "dis-ease" of the majority of human beings. I believe that the root of this dis-ease is our Addictive Personality. Many people have approached addiction from the outside in: describing the behavior and then trying to stop it. I suggest a reversal to this approach and to view addiction from the inside out: identifying and then changing the thoughts and beliefs that led us into the addictive experience and lifestyle.

While researching this book, I read extensively on the biological basis of addiction, including brain chemistry. I am fascinated with this subject and feel the field holds tremendous promise. However, although I think there is much to be learned, as well as many applications of biologically based approaches, my work is focused on shifting our perception of ourselves and the world. I think of my work as the emotional, cognitive, and spiritual thread that can create healing regardless of biology.

As with any approach, there are pros and cons. I feel that the disease concept, brain research, and possible genetic predisposition for addiction are all useful, regardless of future confirmation or rejection of the scientific validity, because a key to healing is reducing guilt and shame. In early healing, the disease concept allows the individual and family to let go of some blame, condemnation, judgment, and guilt. If saying a person's addiction is a disease or is biologically based allows that individual to look within and say, "I have a choice now as to how to live my life," then I am all for it. Conversely, I have seen many people with addiction problems avoid taking responsibility for their actions and life by blaming all on having a disease they can't do anything about. Therefore, I put less emphasis in my work on the biological aspects of addiction, and more on how to create choice and growth. This is not dismissive of biological approaches, but rather is reflective of what I believe is my best contribution. If, at a minimum, I can assist you in being able to say "I know more about addiction, and happiness, and I have a choice as to how to live my life," I will be satisfied. What I hope for is that this material will introduce positive choice into a life where there has been much suffering.

Is There Really an Addictive Personality?

I realize I may have written a book on healing something that some people will argue does not exist. There is evidence on both sides of the argument, including: there is no addictive personality; the traits associated with addiction are the result of becoming addicted to something; and an addictive personality not only exists, but is the cause of most addictions. To further complicate matters, there is much evidence to support how cultural values, social values, situational factors, emotional and cognitive bias, psychological factors, biological factors, and developmental variations all contribute to addiction.

I believe there is an Addictive Personality within each and every one of us. It is part of being human. Because each of us has the propensity (to greater or lesser degree) to make the mistake of adopting certain beliefs and traits that lead us into some avoidance of suffering and pain, most of us, at some time in our lives, look outside of ourselves for happiness. There are some who tend to do this much more than others. For our purposes, think of the Addictive Personality *not* as something you either have or don't have, but rather as a continuum. This is similar to my view on health in general. The question is not whether we are healthy or unhealthy, but rather where we are on the continuum. Thus we need not waste time deciding if we do or don't have an Addictive Personality. This approach puts the emphasis on recognizing how the belief system of the Addictive Personality keeps us, to varying degrees, from having the full and rich life we want and can claim.

We are all prone to addiction, individually and culturally, yet some of us are more prone than others. The value of my approach is in seeing that healing is not just stopping an addiction, even though this is obviously important. Healing is really about coming to see how the thought system of the Addictive Personality affects our life, and doing the work to adopt another way of being in the world. We, individually and as a culture, need to address not only our specific addictions and addictive lifestyle, but we need to heal the roots of the addictive quest that are within us.

How to Use the Power of Choice to Heal

Although the Addictive Personality will try and convince us that following its lead offers us a multitude of choices, all of the choices it offers have one thing in common: The Four A's. The choices are always some form of what you want to achieve, acquire, accomplish, or seek approval for. Thus, *the Addictive Personality actually only offers us choices on how to further deceive ourselves.*

In my work, as well as in my general outlook on life, I have tried to take a road different from the one to which we are directed by the Addictive Personality and the Four A's. This is not always easy, as our culture is largely supportive of these "choices" because they often bear the trappings of success. For example, most of us were given assignments in school with such instructions as "compare and contrast," or "give a critical analysis." While these skills can have value, their overuse reveals only a partial and limited picture. When we try to analyze or compartmentalize someone or something, we miss their true nature. A common mistake when we approach growth, change, or new experiences is that we try to make a square peg fit into a round hole. To make it fit, we must cut off the corners. Unfortunately we do this with ourselves and the people in our lives. In contrast, when we see commonalities and similarities between ourselves and others, even though they are sometimes painful, we feel more love and connectedness.

Your Teacher Is Standing Right in Front of You

In the 2006 movie *Crash*, a bigoted and troubled police officer stops an African-American professional couple and proceeds to act toward them in abusive ways. Later we see the officer heroically save the woman from a burning car. As both characters struggle to extend their arms to reach each other to find safety, metaphorically and in reality, crisis has brought healing through dealing with each other in the immediate moment and letting go of the past.

It is my belief that we are all teachers and students of one another, and that we are never finished in either role. In a way similar to the movie scene described above, over thirty years ago a great teacher came to see me disguised as a patient. I was an intern at a community counseling center when Tom came to see me. The consulting rooms were quite small, and as Tom entered the room, the smell of urine filled the air. Tom looked and smelled like he had not bathed in three months. In our first session Tom did little else but alternate between blank stares and hysterical laughter. He was missing most of his teeth, and his mouth was dry and cracked. His dirty, matted hair hung down over his unshaven face. This was early in my career, and I had had little experience with patients who didn't in some way resemble me and my upper-middle-class upbringing. Tom had grown up with a mother who had punished him regardless of what he did. He had never received a positive message from her about anything. Tom's father had left when Tom was five. His mother told him that his father's leaving was his fault. Tom's mother was a domestic worker who was frequently fired, causing them to have to move from one transient hotel to another. Again she blamed Tom: "If I didn't have you, I wouldn't have any of these problems." The accumulation of negative messages had paralyzed Tom.

To be honest, I was afraid of Tom. It wasn't that I thought he would hurt me; I was just afraid of his difference. During that first session I saw no similarities between Tom and myself. I met later that week with my supervisor and other colleagues to get their opinions. They were helpful, but I still felt fear and dreaded being in the same room with Tom. I saw Tom three times a week for the next month, but things did not seem to get any better, and I thought perhaps I should refer Tom to someone else. Yet I knew that he had already been bounced around the mental health system after being diagnosed with borderline personality disorder and was seen as an uncooperative patient. So despite the misgivings I felt, I stuck it out with Tom.

Sometime during the second month of therapy, a miracle occurred. *I define a miracle as a shift in perception that allows a person to experience peace and belonging where conflict and separation once existed.*

Instead of going over case notes and trying to figure out what was "wrong" with Tom and how I was supposed to "fix" him, I sat in quiet with my eyes closed and searched for insight in my work with Tom. As I walked into the waiting room to greet Tom, I began to feel intense loneliness. As Tom sat down our eyes connected, and I saw my own isolation and despair in his eyes. This was the thing I most feared. I had focused on how different he was from me, but what I was afraid of was how he was just like me. For most of my life I had repressed my deep sense of loneliness. Though to an outside observer I would probably have appeared "successful," at that time I did not feel this way. I almost always felt a sense of being on the outside looking in.

In a moment our differences melted away. We sat in the nakedness of who we were. During the session he still laughed in his odd way, and he still smelled like urine, but the feeling in the room had changed. The focus had shifted from my being aware of our differences to my being aware of our commonality. In the following sessions, fear left and compassion entered. Critical analysis left and mutual trust grew.

Tom and I spent a few hours together each week for about a year. During that time he was able to tell me about his painful family history and the isolation of his existence. His blank stares and hysterical laughter gave way to tears of both pain and joy. Little changed in his appearance, yet there was an inner change. I will never forget our last meeting. We stood in the middle of the room, embracing for several minutes. During this time I was aware of nothing but my compassion for Tom and our journey together. He stepped back, grinning with his toothless smile, and said, "Now you smell like me." We both laughed. Somehow smelling alike was a fitting way for us to part.

My experience with Tom brought home a few key points that I have continued to make an effort to remember in my daily life.

- When I am focusing on differences, it is often because I'm afraid of something in myself.

- Dwelling on differences creates distance, increases fear, and perpetuates suffering.

- Concentrating on commonalities develops compassion and understanding, and increases love.

- When I am judging another person, it is a good indication that it's time to look at what I am denying about myself.

- When I become attached to fixing or changing another person, rather than accepting and extending compassion to them, I enter into the world of addiction by seeing my happiness as dependent upon another person's behavior.

Who We Are Versus Who Our Addictive Personality Tells Us We Are

The addictive lifestyle that is created by the Addictive Personality is a continued compulsive external search, despite the fact that such a pursuit always leads us into suffering and conflict. This is the way of fear, which is the foundation of the Addictive Personality. This is an essential point to understand: Fear is always what fuels the Addictive Personality, even if we are unaware of the fear. Thus, if we are to heal the Addictive Personality, we must challenge the fundamental fear-based concepts it is built upon, which almost always have some ingredient of guilt and shame, and always increase fear.

> **Guilt.** Guilt is the belief that we have done something wrong, bad, and unforgivable. Guilt is based upon the belief that the past is inescapable and determines the future.

> **Shame.** As guilt increases, we not only believe that we have *done* something bad, we begin to believe that we *are* bad.

Because of guilt and shame and the resulting feelings that we have *done* something wrong and *are* something wrong, we then become plagued with fear. This fear is often not experienced directly because it is masked by our addictive pursuits.

Guilt, shame, and fear leave us with anxiety and feelings of emptiness, incompleteness, and hopelessness. But, the Addictive Personality distracts us from self-examination and leaves us to believe that our inner guilt and shame are so strong and pervasive that we could not possibly get beyond them. So we begin to look to people, places, activities, and possessions for our happiness. It is in this external search that we take our first steps toward addiction.

When I was fifteen my father took my brother and me out to lunch at a nice restaurant near our home. He seemed preoccupied and a bit nervous because this was the day he had chosen to tell us that my mother and he had decided to get a divorce.

Given the state of my parent's marriage and the frequency of their arguments, an objective observer might have thought that this announcement would be no surprise. Yet it was a shock. As I heard the words come from my father's mouth I felt as though the world were ending. Immediately I felt responsible, guilty, ashamed, and afraid. At the time I was probably most aware of being afraid. I don't remember showing any of these feelings to my brother, my father, or anyone else. I kept them well hidden. In a strange way I felt as though I had let my parents down, that somehow I could have done something to prevent their problems.

Given a choice, I probably would have chosen to live with my mother. But I felt as though I had no choice, that I had to live with her because my father had abandoned me. In healing our relationship, my father and I have talked of this period in our lives many times in recent years. He is quite sure that he said that if I wanted to live with him I could. Though it is certainly possible that he did in fact say those words, the message that I heard from him was, "I am done with the family. I have my life to live. You stay at home and take care of your mother. Don't bother me." My brother, who was seventeen at the time, decided to move to Lake Tahoe. I didn't share my feelings with my mother because I felt that she was either emotionally unavailable or hysterical, and that my problems would either further distance her or push her over the edge. Because I made this assumption, I never let my mother know of my internal pain. In retrospect, it would have been healing not to have based my choices on the possible reaction of others, and to let them know how the situation was affecting me.

The result was that I felt empty and alone. At the time, I was attending a private high school. My grades fell because I was often absent. I had already experimented with drugs, but my drug use increased. I was looking for some way to relieve the pain that I was feeling. Shortly after my parents' separation I was called into the headmaster's office. He told me that although he had never permanently expelled a student before, he had decided there was really no hope for me. With the dubious honor of being the first to get kicked out of my school, my guilt and shame only increased.

It wasn't that I just felt guilty and ashamed, I was also terrified of really looking at any aspect of what I was experiencing. I was afraid that by being expelled from school I was worthless and doomed to failure. My guilt, shame, and fear made me feel lonely, empty, and hopeless. I certainly didn't feel worthy of love. As a result, I turned to drugs for relief from the pain of despair.

The following text is from *A Course in Miracles*. For our purposes here, I have replaced the word "ego" with "the Addictive Personality."

> *Love and guilt cannot coexist,*
> *and to accept one is to deny the other.*
> *The end of guilt will never come*
> *as long as you believe there is a reason for it.*
> *For you must learn that guilt is always totally insane,*
> *and has no reason.*
> *Only your mind can produce fear.*
> *You must have noticed an outstanding characteristic*
> *of every end that the Addictive Personality has accepted as its own.*
> *When you have achieved it,*
> *it has not satisfied you.*
> *That is why the Addictive Personality is forced to shift ceaselessly*
> *from one goal to another*
> *so that you will continue to hope*
> *it can yet offer you something.*

The Truth about Happiness

In the last few years I have been pleased to see a significant increase in the amount of research done on what makes us happy, both in the fields of psychology and economics. The results confirm what spiritual traditions and humanistic and existential psychology have always promoted: having more does not make us happier and can actually make our lives less satisfying. One of the key findings of this research is that once our basic needs are met, more money and material possessions don't bring us more happiness. In terms of understanding the Addictive Personality these findings are extremely important, because if we were not culturally entrenched in an addictive lifestyle, these findings would be enough to have us shift our focus to a more giving and inward journey to find true happiness. In other words, we would take the factual information and do two things: we would do what we can to eliminate poverty in the world, and we would focus on a path of inner discovery of love and compassion. Obviously, this has not yet occurred, and is further evidence that as the grip of addiction tightens, individually and culturally, we continue to cling to the same erroneous beliefs despite the evidence to the contrary. If we could see clearly the many negative effects our addictive lifestyle has, both globally and personally, it would become clear that healing the Addictive Personality is imperative not only for our individual happiness, but for the survival of the planet.

With any honest examination there is no denying that the search for external happiness is pervasive in contemporary society. You can't watch more than fifteen minutes of commercial television without a series of advertisements telling you that you need some new and improved products in order to be happier. The average kid in America is exposed to 40,000 commercials per year, and we wonder why they grow up with Addictive Personalities. The core of the addictive lifestyle often begins in childhood when we are most vulnerable to the idea that we are fundamentally inadequate as we are and need something outside ourselves to make us whole.

In my work with countless people with addiction problems, I have often been amazed at the strength and irrationality of the thought system of the Addictive Personality. Once I was giving a lecture about happiness, when I began to notice people were either shaking their heads or looking angry. I asked a woman in the front row why she was shaking her head. She said that she thought I was nuts because I was talking as if people could be happy whenever they wanted, and that was simply not true. A man in the back agreed with her, stating that certain situations were beyond our control and that in such circumstances it would be "natural" to be angry and unhappy. I began to see the absurdity of the thinking within the Addictive Personality. We argue for our unhappiness (and our addictions) as if they were things that we want and need! We convince ourselves that it is the situation rather than our thoughts that determine our experience.

Instead of continuing with the planned lecture, I went on to conduct an impromptu poll. I asked how many people thought that it was possible to be happy all of the time. No hands were raised. I pursued my line of questioning and asked, "What about 80 percent of the time?" A few people raised their hands. "Do I hear 60 percent? How many people think that it is possible to be happy a mere 60 percent of the time?" A few more hands went up. As I continued, the largest group of people raised their hands at the 50 percent mark.

I'll let you in on a secret: When you were born into this world, there is no stamp, tattoo, contract, or other binding paper that states "This new being is limited to 52.31 percent happiness."

The only limitations on your happiness are the ones that your Addictive Personality invents.

For many of us, this is hard to accept. It is much more convenient to place the responsibility on something or someone else than it is to take personal responsibility for our happiness and peace of mind. I invite you to ask yourself a question and give it some thought: What do I need, that I don't have, in order to have peace of mind right now? Using the thought system of the Addictive Personality we would have an endless list: perhaps more money, a more attractive mate, a better job.

That said, at different times in my life I have had situations arise that I felt were most definitely limitations on my happiness. I have learned that these situations are limiting only to the extent that I perceive them to be. Some of the most difficult of these situations have been physical challenges, which have been many.

One of these challenges began years ago when I began to notice that I could not hear as well as before. After a series of tests, the diagnosis was unclear and the prognosis was vague. All the physicians could tell me at the time was that my hearing would probably not get better, might stay the same, and could get progressively worse. I became depressed at the possibility of going deaf, even though I could still hear pretty well. At the time, it was early in my career as a psychologist. I believed that my ears were to me what hands were to a pianist. I feared not being able to function in what I had trained so long to do. I saw the prospect of losing my hearing as a limitation to my happiness and success.

But after looking very closely at my situation, I decided to concentrate on letting go of the negative image of losing my hearing and instead put my energy into thoughts about my hearing loss that were healing. At the time I was relieved, and even proud, that my hearing stabilized and I had no further loss. I went on in my profession and never felt that my hearing limited me in any significant way.

Some time later, however, I fell out of remission and had a sudden profound hearing loss; I could no longer hear my patients, talk on the phone, or function in my college teaching position. I felt that this was indeed a limitation on my identity and happiness. I thought if I couldn't hear, then I couldn't be myself or be happy.

Years later, after losing nearly all of my hearing, it became clear that the cause was an autoimmune disease, so I underwent steroidal and chemotherapy. Hearing aids help somewhat but not that much. Initially my Addictive Personality had a hard time with the fact that I needed to wear them. I was attached to being "healthy and normal."

Slowly I began to understand that the real healing that needed to take place was in my mind. My task was to find the lesson in what was occurring. In short, I needed to come to believe that it was possible to be deaf and happy.

One of the silver linings of my hearing loss has been the discovery that there are far more ways to hear than simply through understanding words. I am now more aware of hearing with the "ear of the heart." I pay more attention to the "sounds" of love, pain, joy, and despair that lie beneath and beyond the content of words. I honor the internal voice of my intuition more than I used to. I have learned that what I once experienced as a total limitation is quite possibly a gift. I am grateful for all of the other levels of hearing that I am learning. There are times when I feel frustrated and sad about being deaf, but I am now able to catch myself and see that the only limitations my hearing loss placed upon me are ones that I invent. I choose to identify with the lessons to be learned rather than the limitations to be invented.

Three Healing Words: "I Am Enough"

It is crucial to question the belief system of the Addictive Personality. Without doing this we cannot have any lasting peace of mind, nor will we be able to solve many of our global environmental issues. In contrast with the Addictive Personality, the Truth-Based Personality tells us that our natural state of mind is one of wholeness and peace.

There is no shortage of love, despite what we may have believed. When we perceive ourselves as separate and alone in a world where there is only so much to go around, we encourage our never-ending quest to try to get "enough," known as the deception of the addictive lifestyle. By contrast, the Truth-Based Personality recognizes a simple fact:

I lack nothing in order to be happy right now.

Some years ago there was a popular musical, *The Little Shop of Horrors*. Perhaps unintentionally, the author provided a powerful and comical example of the Addictive Personality in action. As the story opens, a young man finds a small and unusual plant, which he begins to nurture. One day the young man accidentally cuts his finger and finds that the small plant thrives on his blood. Wanting to keep the plant healthy, he continues to feed it blood, but the plant wants more and more. The bigger the plant grows, the more it wants. The plant is never satisfied and only becomes louder and more obnoxious with increased feeding. Eventually the plant is a monstrous piece of botany demanding, *"Feed Me! Feed Me!"*

Although this example is comical in the context of entertainment, the reality of the addictive lifestyle can be catastrophic. I believe that as a psychologist I have an opportunity to contribute to a solution to a very broad individual and societal problem. It begins by asking: When and how did the Addictive Personality start? This is a question that is of obvious importance and much debate. After many years of practice and reviewed research, I believe the answer is fairly straightforward.

The Addictive Personality began precisely at the moment
when we began to view ourselves as something other than
whole, loving beings.

It is a premise of this book that the experience of peace is not something to be achieved; it is to be remembered. "Who I am (love) has never left, but it has been covered up by the Addictive Personality and addictive lifestyle." You did not become incomplete at some point in your life, you simply forgot who you were, and so began the addictive behavior of searching outside of yourself for happiness. Part of healing this is to realize:

Peace of mind is not something to be "achieved."
The memory of truth is only a thought away.
Love awaits only my welcome.

For years I referred to myself as a recovering addict and used the phrase "in my recovery" to preface some conversations. One day, as I listened to myself, my words began to sound like fingernails screeching against a blackboard. At the time I wasn't sure why it bothered me so much. Eventually, I began to make sense of it. Today, I don't see myself as a "recovering addict" as much as I see myself a "remembering human being." For me, though the word *recovery* positively reminded me that healing the Addictive Personality is an ongoing experience, it also somehow put my wholeness out in the future someplace. In contrast, the word *remembering* reminds me that love has never abandoned me, it has been covered up with layers of the addictive thinking. Now when I refer to myself as a remembering human being, I am reminding myself that:

> **True healing is simply to remember I am whole and complete right now.**

Denial: The Not-So-Little Secret

I am an amateur magician (my daughters, who have endured the same tricks for years, would emphasize the word "amateur"). The common element of most tricks is to direct your audience to look where you want them to, which is never at the source of the real action. This is how the illusion is maintained and not discovered. Similarly, in order for the Addictive Personality to believe something that is not true (i.e., you need something outside of yourself to be happy, complete, and whole) there needs to be a mechanism to keep us from seeing the truth. This mechanism is denial.

The word *denial* is used frequently in any full discussion of addiction. This is because it is difficult to address a problem if you do not see that there is a problem. The addicted mind uses its ability to deny and delude to its full advantage. To the person who is looking at another person's obvious addictive behavior, it can be baffling that they don't simply see their addiction and do something about it. So to understand denial, we must understand that it is a central part of what keeps the Addictive Personality intact. I, for example, can recall years of engaging in denial. The denial system of my Addictive Personality kept me in an irrational frame of mind, allowing me to continue and escalate my addictions. Regardless of the plentiful evidence that my life was not working well, I convinced myself that I was in complete control and had no problems at all. (I will discuss this in more depth on page 35, "How the Addictive Personality Uses the Past and the

Present to Prevent Positive Change," but for now it is important to see the basic purpose of denial.)

Denial is multilayered. Our denial mechanism is not really in place only to deny addictive behavior. *The full purpose of the denial system of the Addictive Personality is to deny our underlying wholeness.* In other words, with any addiction, in order for the Addictive Personality to continue its obsessive quest for external gratification, our underlying wholeness must be denied. Simply put, the Addictive Personality cannot exist where love and wholeness are truly acknowledged. This can be realized by asking ourselves the direct question: If I fully believed I was whole and that all love was available to me each and every moment, how would I live my life? The answer is simple: If we experienced ourselves as whole, addiction would not occur, because we would already feel complete. We would concern ourselves with making the world a better place by extending love and compassion rather than trying to get more of something we don't really need. Unfortunately, because of denial we remain blind to our own addictive patterns and the fallacies of our Addictive Personality. Thus, in healing we need to make a conscious and continuous effort to undo denial.

> Addiction is born out of thinking that we are less than whole.
> Today let me not see myself as limited in any way.
> Today may I stop denying the real and beautiful truth
> about who I am.

The Addictive Personality's Plan: Deny It and It Will Disappear

The Addictive Personality's backward plan for our release from guilt has two key elements: denial and projection.

In the early 1980s, I was living on a ranch about thirty miles north of San Francisco. The only utility service on the ranch was electricity. Water came from a spring. Accumulated trash needed to be recycled, hauled to the dump, or composted. I was in charge of the compost pile. For convenience, I chose a spot for it near the house. About once a week, I would take the organic garbage out and put it in the compost pile, diligently breaking up the larger pieces and mixing them into the earth. As time went on I became lazy and sometimes I just buried some of the larger pieces, not taking the time to break the material apart and combine it into the soil. One day, while I sat reading in my favorite spot, I noticed the place was starting to smell like a dump. My laziness in just burying my garbage had ruined my ability to relax and enjoy my peaceful spot. A farmer I am not, but I did learn one simple rule: burying something and forgetting about it does not necessarily make it go away.

One aspect of denial is thinking that if we bury our guilt by pushing it out of our awareness, we will be free of it. Not unlike my laziness with the compost pile, denial does not get rid of guilt. Denial produces an increasingly palatable level of anxiety. Ultimately, denial comes from, and reinforces, fear.

Projection: The Illusion That Keeps on Rolling

When you try to deny guilt, it inevitably starts eating away at you, making it impossible to relax and be at peace. Then you look for other ways to get rid of it. Projection is when you unconsciously project your guilt away from yourself and onto someone else so you will magically be freed. But instead, your feelings of guilt, fear, and inadequacy continue to increase.

This may be a difficult concept to grasp at first, not because it is complicated, but because we may have become accustomed to projecting our guilt onto someone else. By so doing we think that we are safe from our most hidden fears. The problem is that this process of projection keeps us from looking at the source of the problem: the Addictive Personality.

Projection, and the behavior that is a result of it, is best illustrated with a metaphor. Imagine that we set up a movie projector in order to view a film. The lights dim and the film begins. About ten minutes into the movie you notice that I am fidgeting and appear uncomfortable. You ask me if I am okay, and I tell you that I don't like the movie, in fact, it is making me very uncomfortable. You know me as a rational person, so what I do next surprises you. I get up, walk over to the screen, and try to rip it. I don't like the movie, so I try to change the screen. There is little doubt you will quickly conclude that I am acting crazy.

I suggest to you that each of us, sometimes on a daily basis, exhibits this insane behavior, but because we have a lot of company, nobody ever questions it. So let's question it now. If you don't like the movie, what are your more sane options? Though there are several answers, probably the most rational would involve turning off the projector or changing the film. These answers reflect an understanding that the source of the image is not the screen. The image is projected onto the screen.

To understand how projection works in your daily life, imagine that the film projector is your mind and the film is your thoughts. By seeing life this way we begin to recognize an important fact that we must embrace if we are to find peace of mind.

What you see is your own state of mind projected outward.

The Addictive Personality uses denial to keep you from seeing this fact. By projecting, you may believe that if you change other people or situations to meet your specifications, then you will be happy. However, this is the same as my walking up to the movie screen and trying to change it. Another way to see this is to remember how I said a magician always misleads in order for you not to see the trick. In the same way, when we see negative things in other people it is often because our Addictive Personality is directing our attention to an illusion and away from what it does not want us to see. In an effort to rid ourselves of what we don't want to look at in ourselves, we project it onto another person.

Although on an intellectual level I understand projection, at times I still find myself acting insanely: trying to change others or seeing my dark side in them. For example, at one time, President George W. Bush was considering escalating our troops in Iraq despite a bipartisan committee suggestion that he admit to making a mistake by starting the war in the first place, and decrease the number of U.S. troops. I became upset because I felt that the president was unwilling to take responsibility for his errors in judgment and do something other than follow his original, erroneous course. In the middle of a self-righteous tirade to a friend, I realized how many times in my life I had done the same thing I was accusing the president of doing. How often, in even my closest relationships, have I made mistakes? But when challenged, rather than look calmly at my past behavior and admit my transgressions, I became more defensive and argumentative. I bring this up because healing the Addictive Personality involves developing the maturity to make even those we are in conflict with our teachers. In this example, President Bush became my teacher, allowing me to see how I still fall into projecting, denying, and becoming defensive.

Sam Keen, in his book *Faces of the Enemy*, eloquently describes this process of creating images of the enemy out of our own repressed darkness. What he states about world conflict is also applicable to interpersonal conflict. According to Keen, "Healing begins when we cease playing the blame game, when we stop assigning responsibility for war to some mysterious external agency and dare to become conscious of our violent ways."

When you blame another person for your unhappiness, it is a good indication that it's time to look at yourself and accept the responsibility that you have the ability to shape your own life. If you cling to the habit of blaming others, you create a split between the conscious image of yourself as good, and your unconscious image of yourself as bad. *The greater the split between the conscious and unconscious, the greater the need to project, and the greater the suffering.*

Projection can seem complex, but it is really quite simple. A few years back I adopted a new playful puppy. He would run from room to room, playing with whatever he found. One day I heard him fiercely barking and growling, something that I had never heard him do before. When I found him he was in the bathroom; the door had partially shut, revealing a full-length mirror. He was standing there, feet firmly planted, hackles raised, growling at his image in the mirror. I thought it was pretty silly of him not to realize he was threatening to attack his own image. But I realized that a lot of the time I am just as silly. I growl at others, not realizing that I am seeing repressed parts of myself.

Special Hate and Special Love Relationships

The Addictive Personality fosters two kinds of relationships: special hate and special love relationships. These can also be thought of as the two forms of projection.

In a special hate relationship the Addictive Personality creates a stage to play out the blame game. We take our own self-hatred, remorse, guilt, shame, and fear, and transfer it onto another. The goal of the game is to make someone else responsible for our misery. In the special hate relationship we also play the game of hot potato, where anything we don't want to look at we quickly "throw" to the closest available target.

Special love relationships may seem to be more appealing, but they really have the same goal as special hate relationships: to get rid of guilt and shame. In the thought system of the Addictive Personality we feel incomplete and needy. Everything we perceive to be lacking in our lives can never be healed or filled from within. So we begin to search for people, situations, or substances that make us feel complete, even temporarily. Special love relationships are relationships of conditional love: "If you fill my needs, as I want and expect you to, I will love you. If you fail to do so, my love will quickly turn cold." I feel that this expectation is responsible for most relationship and family problems.

When I was growing up, my parents demonstrated their love in ways that felt conditional; it seemed to me as though their love depended on my fulfilling specific expectations. This is not uncommon in families, but the effect can be so isolating.

For example, my father's evening routine was very predictable: home at 6:20 P.M., cocktails immediately with my mother, and then dinner. At the table the dreaded questions would begin, always about what I had done that day. I always wished that I could say something like, "Well, Dad, after receiving the highest grade on the calculus final in the morning, I went on to throw the touchdown pass at the big game in the afternoon and was carried off the field on the shoulders of the entire student body." Unfortunately, my answer was usually, "Nuth'n."

I didn't feel that my dad was asking me because he was really interested, but rather that he was checking up to see if I was deserving of love that day. All those evenings at the dinner table I never felt that my dad was interested in my true feelings. In fact, I felt that he would not have liked it if I had shared them with him. Had I ever been truthful about my average day, I probably would have said, "Well, Dad, most of the day I walked around comparing myself with other people. I felt self-conscious about how I looked. I felt that I didn't quite belong anywhere, as if I were on the outside looking in. In PE I felt like a geek. I almost threw up while doing laps. We are going to have a test in math this week, and I am going to fake being sick because I don't understand anything and am afraid of failing. After school I smoked a couple of joints with some friends."

I never actually understood what my father did or how he felt. I knew he was a psychiatrist, but I wasn't really sure what that meant. On a feeling level, I did know that my dad had two modes. I was aware when my dad was approving and when he was angry. I saw my job as seeking the approval and avoiding the anger.

As I write this, I am thankful for the healing that has taken place between my parents and myself in my adult years. My mom is still living but, sadly, has severe dementia. My dad is in his eighties and going strong. I can now let him know how I am feeling at any time, and I now know his intention is to be accepting of me. Getting to this place with him required that I take the risks of opening up and being vulnerable. We hadn't really known each other before. Each of us had to choose to share our pain in order to let go of it and move to forgiveness. The following is an excerpt from a letter I wrote that was previously published in our book *Listen to Me*.

> *Dad,*
> *I have hidden from and fought you; I have left you, pushed you,*
> *and tried to rise above you; I have idolized and demonized you; I*
> *have blamed, loved, and hated you; I have judged you, run from*
> *you, and run to you; I have played and competed with you; I have*
> *lied and raged at you; I have needed you and denied you. Now*
> *all I want is to let you into my life more fully and completely. I'm*
> *grateful you are in my life and I love you very much.*

In closing of this chapter, I invite you to read and practice the following:

Today, allow yourself to recognize that you are whole within.
Silently, within the depths of your Self,
find all that is perfect and complete.

Open your mind to healing
by releasing expectations of yourself and others.

All that you need to know today is that
love is shining in you now.

The Thought System of the Addictive Personality

Take a moment and think about the following statement, for if you are to heal your Addictive Personality and lifestyle, you must first have an idea of what is at the core of all your addictive thoughts and behaviors.

Fear is the fuel upon which the Addictive Personality and lifestyle run.

You are beginning to see that it is your thoughts created by your Addictive Personality that are leading you into pain and addiction, and it is these thoughts that you must heal. *A Course in Miracles* states this beautifully:

> *It is your thoughts alone that cause you pain. Nothing external to your mind can hurt or injure you in any way. There is no cause beyond yourself that can reach down and bring oppression. No one but yourself affects you. There is nothing in the world that has the power to make you ill or sad, weak or frail.*

Although some of us may have a genetic predisposition to addiction, I believe that we are all equally prone to the addictive behaviors and conflicted ways of thinking. I also believe we all equally yearn for wholeness and love, but when we repeatedly make the mistake of looking outside ourselves for peace and happiness we are at the mercy of our Addictive Personality.

Serenity must come from within. It is my belief that there is only one opposing emotion to love, and that is fear. I posit that there are four fundamental parts of the Addictive Personality's thought system. They are fear, living in the past or the future, judgment, and a belief in scarcity. The following diagram illustrates the foundation of the thought system of the Addictive Personality:

Thought System of the Addictive Personality

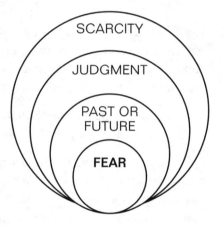

How the Addictive Personality Uses Fear to Control You

Contemplate the following statements:

- When you find yourself turning to a drug, a job, food, a situation, material possessions, or a relationship for your happiness, it is because you are afraid, having forgotten who you truly are.

- When you become like a frightened child, seeing fearsome images in the dark, seeing attack and hostility all around you, your mind has forgotten that you are love, and, in turn, you continue to be afraid.

- When you have an endless résumé of accomplishments and still don't feel good about yourself, truth and peace seem to be nowhere and you are afraid.

- When you want nothing more than to feel the love of another, yet you continually armor yourself with defenses, it is because you are in an ironic dilemma: you are afraid of that for which you yearn.

We try to control these aspects of fear by using projection and denial, which keep us in a world where our fears are constantly reinforced. We end up being afraid of love and freedom. Instead of inviting opportunity into our life we become hosts to guilt. We become like captive birds who never learned to fly, sitting in cages surrounded by bars of fear, forged by our own thinking.

As a child growing up in an alcoholic home, I learned that it was not safe to talk about my feelings in my family so I remained silent, alone with my fears. I went through the early part of my adult life playing out the silent and hidden feelings of my childhood. I always felt as though I was in an unsafe place and was unable to confide in or rely on anyone. I had no real friends through college, and most of my supervisors and fellow interns in graduate school and beyond saw me as bright and capable, but also distant, guarded, and aloof. Although I longed for closeness with the few women I dated, the truth was that trust did not come easily for me. This, combined with my inability to express my feelings, kept me in a constantly lonely and fearful state.

As part of my training as a psychologist I had to go into therapy. Because of my family history, I had a difficult time opening up to the therapist. In the course of our early work together, I think I emerged as a young man who had never felt truly loved. I remember being shocked to discover that there were only one or two photographs of me as a little boy in existence, which made me feel utterly unimportant. As a child growing up in an alcoholic home, I had become fearful and mistrusting; as an adult I knew no other way to be.

During therapy, it became clear that there was a part of me that felt illogically responsible and guilty for what had occurred within my family.

Irrationally, I wondered if I had done something to cause my parents' problems. I also felt guilty for feeling grateful to have had any attention at all. The combination of these factors made me feel that I was not deserving of a loving relationship of any kind. There was no doubt that I was longing for love, yet my fear, guilt, and negative self-image kept me stuck in a cycle of being defensive or isolated or both.

You may be wondering what my personal story has to do with you. I choose to share it here because those experiences sowed the seeds of what became a very strong Addictive Personality. Although there are many ways a person can develop an Addictive Personality, in most cases, the common thread is that we continue to feel guilty, inadequate, and fearful, which leads to isolating, projecting, compulsive and defensive behavior, despite the fact that these behaviors lead to continual unhappiness. This is addiction in the sense that we continue to act and think in the same ways despite the adverse consequences.

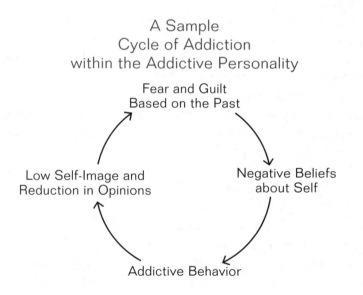

A Sample
Cycle of Addiction
within the Addictive Personality

Fear and Guilt
Based on the Past

Low Self-Image and
Reduction in Opinions

Negative Beliefs
about Self

Addictive Behavior

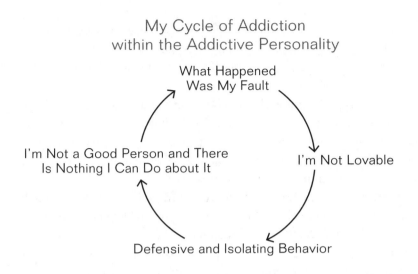

My Cycle of Addiction
within the Addictive Personality

What Happened
Was My Fault

I'm Not a Good Person and There
Is Nothing I Can Do about It

I'm Not Lovable

Defensive and Isolating Behavior

The good news is that I eventually was able to trust my therapist, and, slowly, other people. With a select few I began discussing my feelings about the past and the present. I found myself repeatedly making the choice to allow myself to break the rule of silence I had inherited from my family. This has allowed me to open up with other people on a feeling level and to establish some lasting and honest relationships. As I became less guilt-ridden and fearful, I became less defensive and isolated. I finally experienced real love. As I trusted more, I was able to embark on a spiritual journey that continues to this day. My heart went from being withered, cold, and isolated to full, welcoming, and open. Not long ago I was taking a walk in one of my favorite places. I noticed that I felt different, lighter somehow. I couldn't put my finger on it at first, until it dawned on me —I didn't feel guilty about anything, and there was nobody on the planet that I would be reluctant to run into. I would describe this as freedom. I share this because I would like to help you experience freedom from addiction as well.

How to Break the Addictive Personality's Cycle of Fear

Be aware of your feelings and talk about them. This often requires a leap of faith, because we may think our feelings are silly, are not worth hearing, or will hurt other people. We may think that what is deep inside is so dark and scary that if we even crack open the door even a little, we will be overwhelmed. This fear is so common that it pushes some people further into addiction as a means to keeping the door to the dungeon of darkness sealed shut.

If you don't feel comfortable talking to another person at first, begin by getting a journal and writing down your feelings, including your fears. If you feel that you don't have anyone with whom you can talk, look again. For most people, there really is someone if we choose to look. Therapy can also help start the talking and trusting process.

Identify your irrational beliefs, thoughts, and negative self-talk. The only true statement about yourself is that you are a whole, loving, and fully worthwhile human being. Any statement about yourself that does not reflect this simple truth is an irrational belief about yourself. Any statement other than this keeps you from love and eventually becomes like a weight tied to your ankle.

> There is nothing that you have done in the past
> that makes you unworthy of love.
>
> There is nothing that you need to do to become lovable.
>
> This instant you are not only worthy of love, you are love itself.

Right now you probably have many irrational beliefs about yourself that are keeping you from experiencing peace of mind. Any unforgiving or condemning thought that you think about yourself locks love out. Your Addictive Personality hides this truth and takes each irrational thought and creates a dark and fearful image of itself and seals the door to love. Begin today to take note of your irrational beliefs about yourself, and you will see the absurdity at their core.

Tell yourself there is nothing you want to hide, even if you could. Most of us go through life thinking that there are certain things that we must keep hidden if we want to be loved. We have to bring our fears and dark thoughts up to our full awareness in order to see that they are really based on nothing. Only then can we let them go. It is in releasing our fear that we are healed, not in keeping it hidden.

The escape from darkness involves two stages: First, the recognition that darkness cannot hide. This step usually entails fear. Second, the recognition that there is nothing you want to hide even if you could. This step brings escape from fear. When you have become willing to hide nothing, you will . . . understand peace and joy. (ACIM)

How the Addictive Personality Uses the Past and the Future to Prevent Positive Change

What we think time is for and how we use it determines much of what we experience. From the perspective of the Addictive Personality, the purpose of time is to solidify our guilt and judgment-riddled past and to worry about the future. Looked at honestly, it doesn't take long to realize the resulting experience is not one of serenity, but of anxiety.

For years I used the past to create a stockpile of ammunition to condemn both myself and others. Not a day went by that I did not think about things I had done "wrong" in the past, and I made guilt bombs that repeatedly exploded within me. I held on to past grievances with other people and allowed the anger and resentment to eat away at me. Even the people to whom I was closest did not escape my wrath. In fact, they usually got the brunt of it. I carried around past resentments that became like sandbags, keeping the flow of love out of my relationships. Compounding all of this, I projected my negativity into the future and became not only increasingly depressed but also worried and cynical.

I was convinced that how I saw myself, my situation, and other people were accurate reflections of reality. If challenged, I could easily come up with past incidents to support my beliefs. What my Addictive Personality prevented me from realizing was that everything I was seeing was actually based on my *perception*. Have you ever noticed how two people can experience exactly the same situation but describe them completely differently? This is because of how we choose to perceive the event, and the Addictive Personality will always choose a process similar to what I describe above. This perception is created by how we view time. In other words, constantly looking to the past and worrying about the future is a habit that keeps us from knowing who we are.

Until I direct my mind to let go of the past,
I will not really know myself and happiness and
opportunity will continue to escape my awareness.

And how does the person with an Addictive Personality view the future? The future looks like a black hole of worry. What better way to be distracted than by images of catastrophic possibilities that lie in the future?

I would estimate that the average adult spends much more than 50 percent of his or her time preoccupied with some event in the future. Questions fill our minds: Will I have enough money to pay the bills? What if I fail? Will this person or that person like and accept me? The list goes on and on. Remember:

Every time we become preoccupied with the future,
we create an obstacle for opportunity in the present.
Happiness and opportunity live in the present moment,
absent of the past or the future.

Let's look at the past and the future for what they really are. The conclusion is that, quite simply, the past is past: gone, here no more, nonexistent. The future is not yet here; it exists only in your mind. All of your worrying is of no use; the Addictive Personality keeps you in a state of constant worry that reinforces fear. In fact, worry can actually create what it is you are worrying about. This phenomenon is called a self-fulfilling prophecy.

My grandmother, who died in 1988 at the age of ninety-six, believed that people could not be fully trusted. She believed that if she did not keep a watchful eye on everyone that she would be cheated, ignored, or treated poorly in some way. For years I saw this behavior as moderately paranoid. I knew that my grandmother loved me very much, and I loved her, so I went along with her sometimes bizarre requests, knowing that it would be useless to argue with her.

In her later years she lived in a nice retirement home. On each occasion that I visited her she would tell me how she was being treated worse than anyone else, that she was being ignored, and that she feared that pretty soon she would not be getting any service at all. I assumed that none of this was really so, that it was all paranoia on my grandmother's part.

One sunny afternoon I was out on my deck, which was next door to a restaurant with outside seating. I was watering some plants when an intoxicated woman dining at the restaurant tried to engage me in conversation. At first I tried to just go on watering my plants, but the woman was very persistent. She asked me my name, and I told her, as I continued to water my plants. When she heard my last name, Jampolsky, she immediately said, "Ah, shoot, I take care of your grandma." She was an employee at my grandmother's retirement home.

"Yeah, I know your grandma," she went on. "She's the biggest pain in the butt in the place. We draw straws to determine who has to deal with her that day. She's always suspicious, constantly thinking that we've stolen something. We all keep waiting for it to get better, but it only seems to get worse. I can't believe that lady has a normal relative."

As she droned on, I began to realize that it was not simply paranoia on my grandmother's part. She was, in fact, getting second-class treatment. My grandmother had created for herself what she feared the most, which is what the Addictive Personality always does but will never admit to. She was so worried about being treated poorly that she was cantankerous and suspicious of everyone. In turn, her caretakers avoided her, which confirmed her fears and provided her with "proof" that she had been right all along. This precipitated even more complaints on her part.

My grandmother, bless her heart, taught me a lot about how each person creates his or her own experience. If we project a negative future based on a negative past, the chances are good we will create a negative reality. However, the more we stay focused on the present, the closer we get to being free.

> Here in the present is the world set free. For as you let the
> past be lifted and release the future from your ancient fears,
> you find escape and give it to the world. (ACIM)

There are two very different approaches to creating the life we want. One works, the other does not. As you read this section, keep one question in mind: What are the end results of following the thought system of the Addictive Personality versus that of the Truth-Based Personality?

The Addictive Personality is continually looking for anything it can use to make us feel good, which seems fair enough because we all like to feel good. But, usually, the quest to feel good is actually a retreat from pain. Ironically, the retreat is what, in the end, causes the suffering. Please read the last sentence again because it is crucial to the healing of the Addictive

Personality. It is not always easy to grasp as most of us have been taught that pain and suffering are the same thing, and they are to be avoided at all cost.

Running from pain causes suffering.

The Addictive Personality dictates situations either as "to be avoided because it is painful" or "to be embraced because it makes you feel better." What it does not want you to know is there is nothing about a specific ailment or situation in itself that causes us to experience emotional upset, and that running from the perceived pain is actually the source of the suffering. It could even be said that another definition of addiction is continuing to run from perceived painful situations by ways that temporarily make us feel better, despite an increase in our suffering. In the end, the things we do to make us feel better (drugs, alcohol, shopping, eating, relationships, work, gambling) are what cause our suffering.

Have you ever watched a small child play when his or her parent is nearby? If the child has a minor fall, he or she looks to the parent for a cue as to how to experience the situation. If the parent looks alarmed and runs to the child, the child begins to cry. Alternatively, if, when the child falls, the parent acts like falling is just part of the activity, the child goes on playing. Similarly, when any situation, good or bad, occurs in life we have the choice to experience it with the Addictive Personality or the Truth-Based Personality. How we see the situation and to what degree we experience pain is based on this, and determines our response.

I have an informal theory about how narcotic pain medication relieves pain. When you are under the influence of narcotics, you have a distorted sense of time. Minutes, hours, and, with prolonged use, even days blur together. When this sense of linear time is altered, pain lessens.

A similar phenomenon is seen in many athletes; they can endure prolonged discomfort and still excel in their performance. Perhaps this is at least partially due to the release of endorphins, an opiate-like substance that the body releases during intense exercise. Many athletes report that during their performance, time takes on a different dimension. The present moment seems to be all that exists. Two examples stand out in my mind.

During the 1988 Olympics, diver Greg Louganis repeatedly made perfect dives, even after hitting his head on the board during a dive early in the competition. His injury required stitches, but he was back diving the next day. As he stood at the end of the board preparing for his dive, you could feel the intensity of his focused thought. I am quite sure he was not following the dictates of the Addictive Personality, which would have reminded him of the experience of the previous day and caused him to worry about hitting his head again. Instead, he was fully present, which enabled him to perform at his peak. He went on to win yet another gold medal.

I enjoy the challenge of preparing for and participating in endurance cycling. It has taught me a lot about how to deal with pain and the best ways to perform at my peak level. I have cycled in many countries and have enjoyed each new challenge. One of them was a ride up Haleakala, the 10,023-foot dormant volcano on the Hawaiian island of Maui. The 38-mile road up the volcano achieves the greatest elevation gain in the shortest mileage of any road in the world. This makes the ride very steep and unrelenting. Often the weather at sea level is hot and humid, but the weather at the top is extremely windy and cold. I found the ride to be more challenging than I anticipated and wasn't surprised to see many riders dropping out. At one point I seriously considered quitting. I thought to myself that there were surely better ways to spend one's vacation than enduring this kind of suffering. My legs cramped and I gasped for air, as I looked up at the endless winding road. I thought there was no way I could finish the ride. But instead of giving into this way of thinking, I shifted my focus inward rather than on how far I still had to go. Instead of focusing on my pain, I focused on each breath, on each turn of the crank. Gradually, my awareness of my exhaustion lessened, and I felt that I was in a mild trance-like state. I seemed to become much more inwardly oriented, away from the linear constraints of time and what was left to accomplish. I think I made it to the peak not because of my physical preparation, but as a result of my decision to just be in the present.

I share these examples to illustrate that there is a direct link between one's performance and one's perception of time. If you are coming from the Addictive Personality you will be preoccupied with past failures, and there is little chance of your excelling in what you are doing. This is true whether you are an athlete, a businessperson, or dealing with any challenge. It is also true in relationships. If we are stuck in the past, in telling ourselves how hard the future is going to be, we will never have the relationship that we would like to have.

How the Addictive Personality Uses Judgment
to Maintain Conflict–Centered Relationships

Imagine a world where no one made negative judgments. What a sense of release and total peace would come from meeting yourself and others completely without negative judgment!

Sometimes during a lecture or workshop I will ask the participants, "How many of you would like to be more loving, kind, and happy human beings?" Of course there are no people who say, "No, I would like to be more hateful, cruel, and miserable." Yet, in the Addictive Personality, we create a life in which our judgments get in the way of love. Quite simply, we cannot be judgmental and loving and kind at the same time. When healing the Addictive Personality it is important to remind yourself often that:

> **When you are judging, you cannot love purely.**
> **When you love purely, you cannot judge.**

Think about your own life and of all the times that you have judged yourself or others. Have you ever felt love and judgment at the same time? Look at the judgment for what it is and what it creates. Judgment sentences you to guilt, low self-esteem, and feelings of inadequacy, which are created by and perpetuated by the Addictive Personality. If you constantly compare yourself to others, you can never allow love to set you free.

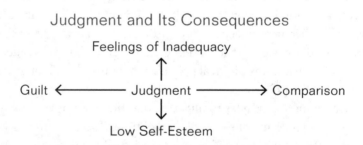

Judgment and Its Consequences

Feelings of Inadequacy
↑
Guilt ←——————— Judgment ———————→ Comparison
↓
Low Self-Esteem

When you look at the Addictive Personality carefully, you see that whenever you make a negative judgment you are making a choice to experience conflict rather than peace. To understand better how judgment affects your life, imagine that whenever you pass judgment you are putting on a pair of sunglasses that filters out love.

Many of us have been taught that judgment and analysis are the hallmarks of knowledge and wisdom. Judgment and analysis are indeed useful tools in scientific experiments, but life is not a scientific experiment. Even scientists have found that reductionism leads to a limited and distorted view of reality. In our personal lives, judgment can hardly be called wisdom. In fact, judgment keeps us from experiencing love. True wisdom lies in the relinquishment of our negative judgment, not in the refinement of our analytical skills.

With today's high rate of divorce, it is painfully apparent that many of us have problems with the relentless grip of judgment squeezing the joy of love out of our relationships. I am no stranger to this. Fourteen years ago, during my divorce with Carny, my mind seemed trapped in a complex web of judgment, both toward her and myself. I blamed myself for the divorce, thinking "if only" I had done things differently. At the same time I blamed her for not being able to commit herself to working on the marriage. This double bind of judgment kept me depressed and angry while at the same time distracted with a constant need to analyze the situation.

During the divorce I found that the more I analyzed the situation, the more I would compare myself with the ideal husband that I wanted to be. This only led to more self-blame. Self-blame quickly led to anger toward both of us. This "analyze-compare-blame-anger" cycle perpetuated my depression and internal conflict. I came to believe that my wife's decision to end the marriage was proof that I was not worthy of love.

I vacillated between judging her and judging myself. For a while I was stuck in the mode of judging her. I believed that if I found fault with her it would relieve my feelings of guilt and self-blame. But judging her was like putting salt on my wound of guilt; it only made my pain worse.

Following the divorce I realized that I was afraid of love and intimacy. As much as we all want intimacy, many of us are afraid of it, as I was. In healing the Addictive Personality I have to continue to address this fear, and I believe it will be a lifelong process of continuing to work on self-acceptance and love. By practicing the principles set forth in this book, I have come to more consistently welcome intimacy instead of running from it. Additionally, in the many years since Carny and I divorced, we both have learned and grown from one another, and we are very good friends today. Our friendship is very important to both of us, and I anticipate that we will always see the importance of maintaining it.

The Peaceful Alternative to Judgment

The peaceful alternative to the Addictive Personality's use of negative judgment is the Truth-Based Personality's use of acceptance and forgiveness. Where judgment builds a wall, keeping love out, forgiveness sends an invitation to love.

> When I have forgiven myself and remembered who I am,
> I will bless everyone and everything I see. (ACIM)

The Addictive Personality uses judgment as a means to set conditions on love: I will love you *if* I find you fit my expectations and *if* you pass my evaluations. A judgmental mind makes lists, often unconsciously, of passing criteria for love. In contrast, forgiveness sets no conditions. Forgiveness simply allows love to be itself.

I invite you to do an exercise to contrast different experiences that come from judging and from extending love. With your eyes closed, picture someone standing in front of you with whom you are currently experiencing conflict, or have in the past. It may be a parent, a spouse, a co-worker, or even someone whom you have made up. Clearly picture the person, then go ahead and let your mind judge them. Think of all the negative things that you can about the person. Think of all the things they have done you don't like. How do you feel as you do this? Most likely you feel anxious, conflicted, and distant. Remind yourself:

I can't judge and have peace of mind at the same time.

Now imagine that you have a rare type of temporary amnesia so that you can't remember anything negative about the past. Instead of judging this person, see him or her as wanting the same things that you do: kindness and compassion. Genuinely wish for the person to be happy. Surround him or her with love. If a judgmental thought arises, imagine that it is burned away by the intensity of your unwavering wish for the person to be happy and free of any of the past pain in their life that may have contributed to their actions. How do you feel as you extend love? My guess is that you feel a sense of release and a sense of peace. This exercise is all that forgiveness is. Remind yourself:

When I extend love, I receive peace.

We are always choosing between the Addictive Personality's use of judgment and the Truth-Based Personality's use of acceptance and forgiveness. With practice we can just as easily choose to fill our minds with peace as we can with the condemnation and judgment of the Addictive Personality.

How the Addictive Personality Uses Scarcity

If research is accurate, and I believe it is, more does not equal happier. And yet, most people in our culture continue to believe they would be happier if they had more: more dollars in the bank, more prestige at work, a bigger home, a fancy vacation. It would appear that the voice of the Addictive Personality is often louder than truth and reason.

This is a result of the Addictive Personality constantly telling us that we are short on something. The addictive philosophy of "never enough" is endless and stems from one core but hidden belief: Scarcity is the notion that we are *always* lacking something. Because of this belief we become caught in endless pursuits to fill this perceived void. Entrenched in the Addictive Personality, we think that our pursuits are valid, yet the cycle that is actually happening is illustrated on the next page.

In healing the Addictive Personality, it is important for us to be able to step back and see this cycle. If we don't, from within the cycle this way of thinking can appear to make pretty good sense, and we will continue to do the equivalent of chasing our own tails. In other words, we escalate in our addictive lifestyle, despite increasingly feeling empty and unhappy.

The problem with the Addictive Personality's scarcity thinking is twofold. First, it is based on a premise that simply is not true. The truth is that in order to be happy right now you must see that you are whole and lack nothing. Second, the Addictive Personality's thirst is never quenched. After you buy the perfect TV, you need to buy the perfect car, and then find the perfect mate, and so on.

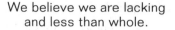

We believe we are lacking
and less than whole.

We embark on a search
for what we mistakenly
think will fill the void.

The Addictive Personality
tells us to search for things
or relationships to make us
feel a sense of wholeness.

We feel even more incom-
plete. And not knowing any
other way to be, we start
the process all over again.

Once recognized for what it is, the feeling of yearning for something more can be positive, as it can be seen as a misdirected spiritual longing. We are like a child who has wandered away from home and become lost. We have wandered away from wholeness and love. In the process we have forgotten who we are and become more lost. The more we have searched outside of ourselves, the more lost we have become. It is only in the quieting of our minds that we can heal this cycle and come to know ourselves.

I remember even after stopping the drugs and undergoing therapy, I still felt like something was missing. I wasn't sure what it was. As I undertook a daily practice of quieting and redirecting my mind, I began to have more insight as to what was going on, and I had experiences of truth. At various times I had an overwhelming sense of peace and calm come over me. These were the first times that I recall ever feeling at ease with myself. It was a new feeling, yet it felt ancient at the same time. Talking and reading can be important in getting ourselves to look within to see what we are doing. But it is in the quiet, beyond the words, that we begin to experience the truth. It is here that we find what we have been yearning for all along: self-love and self-acceptance. This is the purpose of practicing the Daily Lessons beginning on page 145.

The Thirteen Core Beliefs of the Addictive Personality

Entrenchment in the core beliefs of the Addictive Personality leaves us devoid of love, serenity, or true success. (I define success as creating the life we want from a place of wholeness, clarity, and self-worth.) The core beliefs are:

Addictive Personality Belief Number One: *I am separate from everybody else. I am alone in a cruel, harsh, and unforgiving world.*

If you wake up in the morning and are anything less than joyous about the day that lies ahead, you probably have this belief to some extent. The Addictive Personality would have us believe that the world is a place full of judgment and separation, devoid of forgiveness and commonality. When we have this belief of separation, we see ourselves pitted against everything and everyone. If you are operating from this belief, it is only logical that you would build walls and defenses to protect yourself. The only problem is that the belief itself is faulty. Herein lies the irrational logic of the Addictive Personality that "logically" reacts to a belief that is not true, yet never allows the belief itself to be questioned.

When we are born into this world, we are fully open, trusting, and without separation, but the experiences of childhood can teach us to become guarded and untrusting. And so we begin to develop a belief that we are alone, the world is cruel, and most people are not to be trusted. As I review my own childhood, many of my experiences seem humorous today, although at the time they were painful.

One of these tragicomic experiences occurred when I was eight and at summer camp. My brother and I were both a bit reluctant to go, but we were also excited about the outdoor activities. Our first clue as to what was to come was the dramatic shift in the counselors' demeanor as our parents pulled out of the parking lot. Fortunately my brother, who was two years older, became my protector, but even he would be unable to totally shield me from the cruelties of this new world. But before I continue with the story, there are things you need to know: First, our mother, being attentive to camp rules, had sewn nametags onto every piece of our clothing; second, my stomach did not accommodate itself well to camp cuisine; and third, none of these kids seemed to like me very much. These three aspects of camp life combined forces for the worst two weeks that an eight-year-old could imagine.

One afternoon, following lunch, I received an urgent request from my intestines. I snuck out of archery class and ran to the outdoor facilities. Unfortunately, I didn't run quite fast enough and I messed my pants. Not knowing what to do in such a predicament, I quickly changed my under-wear and threw the dirty ones in the garbage. What I failed to take into consideration, however, was, first, the mentality of some of my fellow campmates, and, second, the fact that my action would be detected. To prove just how gross boys can be, one kid, a big guy, found my soiled, *mono-grammed* skivvies and felt compelled to show them to the rest of the camp population. For the remainder of my stay, I was teased relentlessly. To add insult to injury, I had been accidentally hit in the head with a golf club while playing miniature golf. My injury had required a doctor to shave part of my head for the stitches. Having half a shaved head and being known for poop-ing in my pants did nothing to make me more popular. When my parents called, the counselor, who I was sure had a job as a prison guard the rest of the year, told me, in a stern voice complete with heavy accent, to say that we were having fun. Those two dismal weeks were hardly what the camp brochure had promised.

From this experience, combined with others, I built a belief system that convinced me I was alone and unprotected in the world. Much of my addictive lifestyle has been an attempt to avoid my feelings of isolation, poor self-esteem, and shame. Rather than questioning my beliefs about myself, it was much simpler to run from my feelings. I had become addicted to my fears and feelings of aloneness. Only by confronting this addiction could I recognize the truth: that we are all joined and ultimately more "a part of" than "apart from."

Think how different your experiences would be if you knew you were not alone, and that the best defense against isolation was to extend a compassionate hand to another being. Think of all the times you built defenses against loneliness when all you needed to do was offer a kind thought or caring action. When you realize that you've always had a choice between building defenses and extending compassion and understanding, that's when healing begins.

Addictive Personality Belief Number Two:
If I want security and success, I must judge others and defend myself.

The Addictive Personality makes us believe that security and success come from adhering to the following principles:

- Analyze every person and situation effectively, efficiently, and accurately, relying on your past experiences for information rather than the present.

- Use your past experiences and analysis to judge, categorize, and label every person and situation in your life.

- Get all you can, as quickly as you can, because there is not enough of anything to go around.

- Attack anything that you believe may threaten you.

Before reading on, think about how the preceding four principles actually limit your peace of mind, and therefore are really obstacles, not preventative measures, to security and success. The truth is that every time you analyze, judge, categorize, or defend, chances are good that you are not experiencing peace, or creating true success.

Addictive Personality Belief Number Three:
My perceptions are always correct and my way is the right way. To feel good about myself, I must be perfect at all times.

If I had a dime for every time that I was more attached to being right than I was to being happy, I would be a wealthy man. The belief that one is always right is a hallmark of the Addictive Personality, which also believes that being wrong is a sure sign of weakness. Being anything other than right produces feelings of shame because when self-esteem is based upon being right all of the time, being less than perfect is unthinkable.

The extent to which we think we need to be right is the extent to which quality relationships escape us. When we constantly argue and are attached to being right at all costs, we are really arguing for our unhappiness.

Addictive Personality Belief Number Four:
Attack and defense are my only safety.

The cycle of attack and defense is the vicious cycle by which the Addictive Personality sustains itself. If we believe that we are alone in a world where there is not enough to go around, it makes sense to either defend ourselves or lash out in retaliation. Believing that attack and defense are a way to create safety is like throwing a boomerang and thinking that it won't come back. What our Addictive Personality blinds us to is that whenever we attack another, it increases our feelings of being in danger and in need of defense.

Addictive Personality Belief Number Five:
The past and the future are real and must be worried about.

The Addictive Personality is an equal opportunity worrier. We worry about any and all alternatives, thus creating a situation where there is no such thing as a safe future. Compounding the problem, we feel guilty about our past behavior, so our addictive behavior tends to snowball. It starts slowly and over time becomes so strong that it feels like you cannot live without a certain substance, possession, or person. The snowball keeps getting bigger until it seems that it has a mind of its own and we lose control.

Addictive Personality Belief Number Six:
Guilt is inescapable because the past is real.

This belief is an extension of the preceding one, but also operates independently. Much of what keeps us from healing our Addictive Personality and changing our lives is the belief that we have done some acts in the past that are so bad that they are beyond redemption and so keep us feeling guilty. So we remain stuck in shame, lose our self-esteem, and feel totally hopeless.

Over the course of seven years, a former client of mine named Bill had four sales jobs. In each position he was rapidly promoted, and his employers were all very pleased with his work. Despite his successes he never felt good about himself and continued to hope that the next job would be more satisfying. In the course of therapy Bill talked about his career before he became sober. Early in therapy he said that he had worked for one firm for eleven years and that his alcohol and drug use had never affected his job performance. His sales figures were always above average, and he had never been put on probation. Bill described his former employer as being one of his best friends. He stated that they had grown up together and were like brothers. Yet when he first became sober he decided to leave that firm because he thought he needed more of a challenge.

Bill eventually revealed something that he had kept inside of himself for twelve years. On a cloudy December morning, sitting low in his chair, Bill began sobbing heavily. He covered his face with both his hands, attempting to hide the depth of his shame. He told me that twelve years earlier his addiction had cost him more money than he was earning at the time. He had also made some bad investments because his judgment was poor while he was using. Then, through his tears, he confessed that he had embezzled some money from his employer (and best friend) in order to pay his debts and continue his drug use. The amount of money was not large, yet the guilt Bill felt was crushing. In his mind he had done something unforgivable, and therefore his shame was permanent. Quitting that job had nothing to do with wanting more of a challenge. Guilt had caused him to quit. And something he had done twelve years ago was keeping him from having any satisfaction in his work or any other aspect of his life.

As our work together progressed, Bill was finally able to forgive himself. Over the years, Bill and his former boss had become distant, seeing each other only on occasion. Bill contacted his old friend and told him what he had done and that he wanted to pay the money back. To Bill's astonishment his friend said that he had found out about the embezzlement the year after Bill had left. His friend said that he had been very disappointed and angry at the time, but that he had missed Bill through the years. Bill and his friend are back working together, and Bill has at last let go of his guilt.

Addictive Personality Belief Number Seven:
Mistakes require judgment and punishment. They are not opportunities for correction and learning.

Although your Addictive Personality would have you believe that you know how to attain happiness and freedom, the sad truth is it makes you into both judge and jailer. When we are always on the lookout for where we fall short, there is no doubt we will find what we are looking for, and then we will judge and punish ourselves for every mistake. Thus we give ourselves and other people little room to grow. Guilt becomes the glue that holds our relationships together. Guilt, combined with the belief that "My way is the right way," creates internal conflict, stress, and even physical illness. Every minor mistake we make results in judgment and punishment. We make the same harsh judgments about the mistakes of other people, though often secretly. Consequently, we learn little about love and forgiveness.

Although we may pretend to be evolved by acting humble and saying self-deprecating things, this is another form of deception. It is usually an attempt to manipulate another person. Most of us have made a mistake and said something like, "How could I be so stupid!" Yet, calling ourselves stupid, especially if the belittling continues, makes us feel badly and lowers our self-esteem. Eventually, constant self-deprecation can contribute to depression, fatigue, and other physical complaints. In short, over time looking for your shortcomings and self-judgment will suck the zest for life right out of you.

The good news is if we begin to realize what we are doing we will be able to introduce choice on a more consistent basis. Instead of self-deprecating statements disguised as humility, we can say things such as "I'm a worthwhile person. We all make mistakes; this is an opportunity for me to learn." When we do this, our self-esteem naturally goes up. This gives us more energy to do things that we had previously hesitated to do because we feared making a mistake.

It is important not to underestimate the power of your thinking. The truth is that even one negative belief can have pervasive effects on your whole life. Just one belief can keep you from doing the things you want to do. The good news is that reversing just one belief can wake you up to who you really are and what is possible.

Addictive Personality Belief Number Eight:
Fear is real. Do not question it.

The Addictive Personality sustains itself with this belief. As long as we don't question fear, our addictions remain intact. Our state of fear keeps us from questioning the illusory foundation on which it stands. If you want to heal your Addictive Personality, remind yourself of two words: question fear.

Ironically, our fear often increases when we start to look at it. However, it will subside as we recognize its unstable foundation. In fact, in the end, examining our fear is likely to result in an overwhelming sense of relief. When measured against the underlying despair that results from keeping things locked and hidden away, facing our fear is a welcome change.

Over the last twenty-five years I have done a fair amount of public speaking. I enjoy sharing and laughing with groups of people, large and small. This, however, was not always the case.

When I pursued my bachelor's degree, most of my classes were large enough that I could blend in with the rest of the students and not have to speak in front of the class too often. But whenever I did, my heart would pound so hard it seemed it would pound right out of my chest. I was terrified to speak in front of a group and tried to avoid it at all costs.

During my first semester of graduate school, I took a course in ethics that had only twelve students, all of whom appeared to be quite personable. The professor was a kind and soft-spoken man. These facts, however, did not curb my irrational fear of speaking in front of others. In the small group I found myself very uncomfortable. Midway through the class, each student had to give a short presentation. My anxiety escalated as my day approached. Being ashamed that I was afraid, I kept my fear hidden. The day came and I gave my presentation. Never has five minutes seemed more like five hours. It was a truly terrifying experience. My anxiety grew as I pondered how many times I might have to repeat the experience in other classes. Eventually the fear became so great that I dropped out of school, rather than face giving any more presentations.

After leaving school the bottom dropped out of my already low self-esteem. I ended up living alone in a remote small town, relapsing into drug use. I became withdrawn and reclusive. I never felt more alone.

Eventually I was able to become less isolated, but my fear of letting others see who I was persisted, as did my periodic heavy use of drugs. The fear of being known was really what had fueled my terror of speaking in front of others.

After some time, I moved to Seattle, where I later reentered graduate school. I was determined to work through my fear. I chose one very compassionate professor with whom to share my internal struggle. In so doing I took the first step in my healing. Eventually I transferred back to my original graduate school and spent several years of growth there. Working through my fears was not quick or easy, but making the decision to confront my fear rather than run away from it was the turning point for me. I still get a few butterflies speaking in front of others, but I have found that letting others see me as I am is the best way for me to get to know myself. Hiding my fears only makes them grow stronger, because they begin to feed on themselves.

Addictive Personality Belief Number Nine:
Other people and situations are at fault for my feelings and failures.

This is known as the blame game. This belief creates a world where you think that success and happiness are a matter of luck, not conscious choice and attitude. If we find ourself in a "bad" situation, we think that we have no choice but to be unhappy. Any time that you say, "If only such-and-such were different, then I could be happy," you are operating in this addictive belief. Realizing this allows you to begin to heal this addictive pattern by adopting two essential thoughts:

The only person responsible for how you feel is you.
All situations hold the opportunity for you to learn and grow.

If you practiced nothing else in this book other than replacing the habit of blaming with these two new beliefs, your life would be very different *almost immediately*. I invite you to take a moment and think about this. The habit of blaming other people and circumstances for your pain and perceived misfortune can quickly become compulsive. I know firsthand how to convince myself that my problems are a result of someone else's actions. I spent years saying, "If my relationship (job, car, relationships with my parents, and so on) were better, I would be happier." For years I blamed my drug use on everything under the sun, and I probably even blamed the sun once or twice.

In order to heal, you must embrace the fact that the situation does *not* determine your experience. It is your perception of the situation that leads to your attitude, which means everything.

> We each determine what beliefs we want to hold in our mind.
> From these beliefs our experience is born.

Addictive Personality Belief Number Ten:
Another's loss is my gain. Success comes from looking out for number one and pitting myself against others.

With this belief, a fragile self-esteem comes from comparing ourselves with others. When we get caught up in comparisons we are always feeling either superior or inferior to others. Either way we lose, because we overlook any sense of union, connection, or togetherness. Think of the high achiever who appears to have it all, yet feels alone and without love. Though there are certainly many such people who feel good about themselves, there are also many who are caught in the undertow of the Addictive Personality and are workaholics and/or alcoholics. Sometimes the loneliness and despair are so strong that the only option they can see is suicide.

Union, connection, and cooperation are concepts foreign to the Addictive Personality. Instead, you are in a constant battle with your environment, never feeling at ease, always in battle-ready mode, defining success in terms of how many bodies you leave in your wake on your way to the top, and how you compare with others.

Addictive Personality Belief Number Eleven:
I need someone or something else to complete me.

In our quieter moments, even when we are in the grip of addictive behavior, we have the faint underlying feeling that something is amiss, that there must be something more to life than being dragged around by our negative habits and patterns. Properly perceived, this feeling is a spiritual thirst, an internal and deep knowing that there is something larger than ourselves. But when it is repressed, the endless addictive pursuit of looking for happiness outside of ourselves is perpetuated.

I used to believe that I needed something or someone else to be whole, which, ironically, kept me from experiencing true intimacy. What I discovered is that I am capable of intimacy only when I can enter into a relationship fully aware of my wholeness and willing to share openly and honestly who I am. This could not happen as long as I believed that the primary purpose of a relationship was to fill a particular need that I thought I had.

I have also discovered that I cannot experience my own feelings and explore my own self if I am compulsively searching for happiness in possessions, substances, or people. When I return to the memory of who I am, I must make the conscious choice to look within myself. Until I had the courage to take this step I only continued to deceive myself, chasing mirage after mirage and finding only sand.

Addictive Personality Belief Number Twelve:
My self-esteem is based on pleasing you.

"People pleasing" can be an addiction as strong as any drug. In a compulsive quest to please others, we can abandon who we are, losing our sense of self, our sense of identity, except in the context of another person. This belief is part of what I will discuss later as Compulsively-Other-Focused.

It can be confusing: what is people pleasing and what is an act of kindness? The answer depends on your intention and expectations. If you do a deed out of compassion and with a sense of your own wholeness, it is an act of kindness in the light of service. Conversely, if you do the deed because pleasing another or looking good is the only way you can feel good about yourself, or to avoid feeling guilty, you will find yourself in a downward cycle of despair. In short, it is not necessarily the act that determines whether a person is behaving in an addictive way; it is the motivation, attitude, and belief behind the act.

Addictive Personality Belief Number Thirteen:
I need to control everyone and everything around me.

This belief leads us to compulsively trying to manipulate people and situations, which leaves us feeling stressed, anxious, and tense, and believing that the way to control these feelings is to control the world around us. When we fail, of course, we typically experience shame and often react in anger, even rage. We experience no relief beyond temporarily feeling self-righteousness, which allows us to blow off a little steam. But there is always the underlying fear that once in control, we will lose control completely. This need to control people and situations can lead to serious stress-related health problems.

When we hold this belief we often see family members as extensions of ourselves; if a child misbehaves or a spouse dresses in bad taste, we take it personally. We try to make sure that our family members meet certain standards, and when they don't we are once again embarrassed, ashamed, and afraid of the judgments of others. To compensate for these feelings, we sometimes become overly preoccupied with our own achievements: the classic overachiever syndrome.

> The need to control and peace of mind
> cannot occur at the same time.

How These Beliefs Combine Forces

Although it is useful to separately outline the core beliefs above, in real life the Addictive Personality is made up of a few of these core beliefs, in a complicated and often contradictory combination that can be very difficult to make sense of. The purpose of the following story is to illustrate how strong the Addictive Personality can be, but also how it is possible to choose something different.

When the need to control is combined with some of the other core beliefs of the Addictive Personality, the result is often escalating anger, in the irrational notion that our anger will finally control the other person or situation. Living with this toxic combination is agonizing. In the past when people didn't behave in a manner that I wanted them to, I got so angry I used to swear and throw things just to intimidate them. As an adult I have never physically attacked or said belittling things, but I have emotionally exploded and scared those I love most. I acted out of anger in ways that damaged the trust I once had with them. It would be easy to make excuses for myself, because everyone loses their cool from time to time, right? But the truth was that even after years of personal work I was still prone to yelling when I did not get my way. I seemed able to help others with *their* anger, but when I couldn't control my own anger I became secretly hopeless about this aspect of my Addictive Personality.

I was engaging in behavior that was not conducive to creating what I really wanted in my life, and I kept doing it anyway, even when I told myself not to. Though my outbursts were infrequent, I felt weak and ashamed after each one. In response to these episodes, I would either withdraw or escalate in my anger, which is a classic addictive pattern. It was not until I found myself very hurt and yelling in rage one inch from the face of the woman I loved that I knew I had to find another way of being. I suppose I could have yet again listened to my Addictive Personality and blamed my behavior on how hurt I was by her actions, but the truth was I needed to take final responsibility for my thoughts, feelings, and actions.

By this time I had written a few books and had some notoriety, so there was a part of me that felt like a first class hypocrite. Rather than let this overwhelm and stop me, I decided to contact a respected expert on anger to finally do something about this behavior. I could no longer avoid responsibility by saying that "everybody gets angry sometimes." Finally, with help, I saw that behind my anger was a list of "shoulds" and "oughts" that dictated how other people in my life should or ought to act. With such a way of being in the world, only fleeting moments of an extremely fragile happiness were possible. If things were going "right," it was only a matter of time before somebody did something that once again I wanted to try to control.

I had grown up in an environment that was unpredictable; at a moment's notice my world could be turned upside down. As an adult I tried to control other people and my environment in order to make my world safe. None of this is easy for me admit, but I believe my sharing it might help those who have fallen into a similar pattern. The truth is that for years I thought my happiness was dependent on my ability to control other people and situations, and if I can assist you in seeing beyond this or other beliefs of the Addictive Personality, it is worth opening the doors to some of my closets.

Although there was a time in my life when I would have argued that I was not controlling, my need to control had become an addiction to the point that I was acting in ways that were totally irrational. My story illustrates the mid-stages of the addictive need to control another person in order to feel secure. We can easily look to world history to see just how far people will go to control others, even killing millions of people. It is more difficult to see our own controlling behavior, because it typically starts out in small ways. The seeds of controlling behavior can be seen in any statement, belief, or action that suggests a need to control another person, no matter how small and benign it may appear. In even the seemingly benign statements there is still the belief that controlling another person is desirable, and that we should be able to do it. "Shoulds" are essentially the imposition of our needs, beliefs, and values onto others, who may have very different needs, beliefs, and values.

What I have come to realize is the only thing that I am truly in control of are my own thoughts, beliefs, feelings, and behavior. I now have more peace of mind if I see that other people will act how they want to, not according to how I think they should. Stating preferences rather than issuing orders allows for peace of mind. ("I prefer that he not be late" rather than "He should always be here when I think he should be.")

The Two Forms of Communication

The Addictive Personality is a loud and unrelenting voice that never shuts up without a fight. Perhaps you have wondered how you, or maybe someone in your life, could really change. Beneath the Addictive Personality is the quiet, calm, and ever-present voice of the Truth-Based Personality. There is magic about simply having the *intention* to listen to love. It is extending an invitation to what is most true to emerge in your life, and it will.

> The intention to listen to love is a powerful tool.
> Like a river, it will eventually overcome any obstacle.

When you interact with other people operating from the Addictive Personality, their defenses and attitudes may make it seem like they are porcupines: when you try to get close, their quills prick you painfully.

Communication can seem very complicated, yet it is actually quite simple. It is my belief that there are really only two forms of communication. The first is that based on the Truth-Based Personality, where you extend understanding and compassion to yourself and others. The second form of communication is that based on the Addictive Personality; you act defensively from the thirteen core beliefs, yet deep down yearn for love.

In short, the two ways of communication are (1) extending understanding and compassion, and (2) making a call for understanding and compassion. The problem is that calls for understanding and compassion are not always pretty. But if you take a moment and reflect on what you most wanted during the times you were most "prickly," was it not love? When you think about the many ways that people behave that are not what we would deem "friendly," is it not likely that what they really want is understanding and compassion?

Those stuck in the Addictive Personality are so afraid that they build walls around themselves. If they are attacked, the walls will only be reinforced. Taking a jackhammer to the Addictive Personality does not work; *love is the only force that can penetrate the walls of the Addictive Personality.*

But loving does not mean simply being sweet and nice, or tiptoeing around the tough issues. Stating how you feel, in a loving and nonjudgmental way, allows defenses to crumble. What a person with an Addictive Personality is actually saying in so many ways is that he or she is scared and in need of understanding and compassion. Nothing less, nothing more. The more clearly we hear this call for understanding and compassion instead of identifying with the verbal assaults and negative behavior, the greater the opportunity we have of breaking through the walls of the Addictive Personality. This is true on personal, family, and societal levels. The Addictive Personality and lifestyle have wreaked havoc in our lives and the world, and the practice of understanding and compassion is how we can heal.

Some may state that this approach is naïve, and that it can be foolish to see the world in this manner. It is my belief that the expression of love never falls upon deaf ears, even if we don't see immediate results. Understanding and compassion, at the very minimum, begin to open the heart.

The Structure of the Truth–Based Personality

Traditionally in psychology, with the exception of Humanistic and Transpersonal Psychology and the emerging field of Positive Psychology, most all diagnostic procedures begin by looking for what is wrong. The diagnostic manual that most clinicians use is full of descriptions of personality disorders, but no mention of a personality that is highly functioning and at peace, and certainly no mention of how to attain it. I believe that when healing the Addictive Personality it is essential to know what the positive alternatives are and how to adopt them.

The Truth-Based Personality is not so much developed as it is revealed. Imagine a beautiful garden that has been untended and overgrown, that just needs a little clearing and attention to flourish, and you get an idea of the Truth-Based Personality. Think of the Truth-Based Personality as the real truth about yourself, beyond all the fearful thoughts you have created and believe to be true. This truth was never affected by any of your past actions or ways that you lived your life. The Truth-Based Personality is always available for us to tap into and to direct our life.

From a place of peace, the mind allows the warmth of what is true about you to melt away illusions of fear and guilt. We cannot heal our Addictive Personality while we remain entrenched in fear and conflict. It would be like trying to get out of a Chinese finger puzzle: the harder you pull, the tighter it becomes. Trying to get over fear from a place of fear does not work.

In quiet we begin to go
to the depths within ourselves,
finding the memory of love
waiting undisturbed.
Finding love within,
we then begin to share
our fullness with others.

Peace is where love lies waiting,
unharmed by time,
unaffected by the guilt we made
and think is inescapable.
Love is our home,
and it awaits our invitation.

Once we see love within ourselves
we will then see it everywhere.
This is because there simply is no place
that we can look where love is not.

Here is a simple fact that is often overlooked: It is impossible for your mind to serve two goals at once. For example, I may say that I want peace of mind while still holding a grudge over something that happened last week or last year. If I see any value in holding a grudge, my goal cannot really be peace of mind. Peace of mind is impossible as long as we still see value in the fear-based thinking of the Addictive Personality. The Truth-Based Personality asks you to rise above your defenses (the thirteen core beliefs of the Addictive Personality) and accept the invitation to love.

The Truth-Based Personality

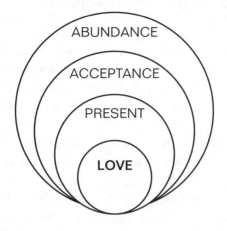

ABUNDANCE

ACCEPTANCE

PRESENT

LOVE

In this chapter the fundamentals of the Truth-Based Personality are presented as the peaceful alternative to living in the continuous conflict of the Addictive Personality.

If you want love,
share.

There is only one way for love to be discovered
and that is through itself.

Offer love
and it will fill the empty spaces of your life
like light entering a darkened room.

As two droplets of water
merging as one,
love is drawn to itself.

But, don't forget,
should you offer attack
and withhold forgiveness,
you will not see
or experience the radiance of love,
for love can only flourish
in a peaceful heart.

How the Truth–Based Personality Uses the Power of Love

Many of us grew up in families, or may currently be in relationships, where the unspoken message is "I'll love you if you do what I want you to do." The "I'll-love-you-if . . ." message causes us to think either that we are undeserving of unconditional love or that we must please others in order to be loved.

Those of us who have received this message nearly always fall prey to the beliefs of the Addictive Personality. We come to believe that if we show anybody all of ourselves, including our dark and hidden thoughts, we will be rejected. Consequently, we keep certain segments of ourselves hidden, in the hope that we can be loved, but secretly we believe if someone really knew us, they would reject us. Addictive pursuits of all kinds are undertaken to push away the resulting pain from living with such beliefs about ourselves.

Often these messages are covert, or have to do with areas that are either not talked about at all, or are only talked about indirectly. The "I'll-love-you-if . . ." message often relates most directly to sensitive issues, such as sex. As a result we can carry hidden guilt and shame for years.

Many of us carry the shame of childhood experiences for years. Although this is very common, we tend to keep such experiences secret. We often repress the memories of these experiences because we feel so ashamed. Our shame in turn makes us feel undeserving of love. When we feel unworthy of receiving unconditional love, we don't feel capable of giving unconditional love; the "I'll-love-you-if . . ." message goes both ways.

Years ago somebody asked me if it were possible, would I be willing to go through one day with a transparent mind. This meant that during a twenty-four-hour period another human being could be aware of my every waking and sleeping thought. At that time this was a frightening thought. I didn't want anybody to know all of what I was thinking for even one minute, let alone a whole day. I was afraid that if people knew my true feelings and thoughts, that I would be rejected in a split second. I believed that if people knew all of what I thought that they would surely see me as angry, hateful, unlovable, and crazy.

The extent to which, due to shame, we keep parts of ourselves hidden from everyone in our lives (and often even ourselves) is the extent to which we are building walls against happiness and new opportunity.

I am not suggesting that we tell every person we meet our deepest secrets. What I am saying is that if we want to discover happiness, we must let go of the need to keep parts of who we are hidden from ourselves as well as those with whom we would like to be close.

When we feel that we must keep aspects of ourselves hidden, in order to be accepted by others, the result is that we never quite feel deserving of any positive experience that we do receive. Groucho Marx once quipped about this feeling, saying "I wouldn't want to belong to a club that would have me for a member." If we want to release ourselves from the Addictive Personality, we must begin to realize that we are fully deserving of happiness and positive outcomes once we begin to align our thoughts and actions with the Truth-Based Personality.

I enjoy finding old wooden furniture that is covered with layers of peeling paint and cracked varnish. When I come across a piece, I try to imagine the beautiful oak, pine, or mahogany that lies beneath. Gently stripping away the layers is a long and tedious job. There are times when the wood actually looks worse than when I started, and I am tempted to abandon the project. Sometimes I need to simply have faith that with a little more work I will see the original, beautiful wood. Once the old gunk is gone, I apply a little oil to the parched, newly exposed surface, and I end up with a gorgeous piece of furniture.

And so it is with moving from the Addictive Personality to the Truth-Based Personality. Do not concern yourself with the layers of fear and darkness, cracked by years of guilt and judgment. Look beneath and imagine the beauty that waits to be uncovered. Know that it is not necessarily going to be an easy or painless process, but that it will be rich in its rewards. When I am done stripping furniture, I don't go through the scrapings of paint on the floor; I throw them all away. They are of no use to me. In the same way, let go of the scraps of memories that are old and guilt ridden and are really not a part of who you are. Admit and learn from your mistakes, but throw away the scraps of shame like old paint. They are of no use to you in the Truth-Based Personality.

As I began to see love in myself I began to see it elsewhere: my daughters' eyes, a friend's touch, even a group of people I had never met; all became reminders of love. During times of challenge I now remind myself that I can see opportunities to love everywhere because they are everywhere. I spent years denying this, but that did not make it untrue. Opportunities to love waited patiently for me to uncover my eyes and open up my heart.

The Addictive Personality tells us that if we look within we will not like what we see, and certainly nobody else will. The first step toward increasing our experience of love is to begin to train the mind to overlook the illusions of darkness (the old paint) created by the Addictive Personality, and welcome what is truly there.

How the Truth–Based Personality Uses the Present Moment to Set You Free

Whenever you are holding onto the past
or worrying about the future,
you are looking nowhere,
seeing things that are not there.

The Truth-Based Personality has a very different clock than the Addictive Personality. Whereas the Addictive Personality uses the past and future to reinforce its negative and fearful views, the Truth-Based Personality uses the present moment to set you free. This very different purpose of time is essentially that in the Truth-Based Personality you go beyond seeing time as linear and instead focus on the present moment. Imagine for a moment how differently you would see yourself and other people if you no longer endlessly rehashed the past, using it as fuel to feed the fires of guilt and anger. You would see yourself and other people in the purity of the present moment, and what you would see would be their true essence.

When we focus on the present, the window of our perception radically shifts. We begin to see the world, and ourselves, in a new light. There is a sense of freshness, release, and relief. There are no measuring sticks to determine self-esteem; there are only truth and opportunity shining in and around you. As we make this shift in our perception of time, a sense of peace enters into our life.

My addictive pattern of thinking went like this:

1. When a situation presented itself I would search my memory to determine if this was a "good" or a "bad" situation.

2. If, on the basis of the past, I deemed it to be good, I would proceed in a way that usually resulted in a "positive" experience.

3. If I decided that it was bad, I would become angry, or upset, and would always have a "negative" experience.

As I looked at this pattern I began to realize an important fact. I had thought that I was reacting appropriately to each situation, when such was not actually the case. What I was reacting to was *my perception* of the situation based on my memory. This is hugely important, because most of us believe we are negatively reacting to facts. We rarely react to facts. It is always our perception that determines our reaction. This becomes obvious when you consider how different people can react very differently to the exact same situation. Until I saw this it had never occurred to me that what *I believed* the situation to be, in fact, determined the experience that I had. I found that I could just as easily create a positive experience as a negative one, regardless of the situation, by choosing to see every situation as an opportunity to learn more about the facets of the Truth-Based Personality.

There are no "good" or "bad" situations.
All situations, even the difficult ones,
are simply opportunities to learn about love.
What we make of each situation is up to us.

Today, rather than engaging in the negative self-talk, I try to do something different whenever I find myself feeling anything other than peaceful. I stop myself and say, "Wait a minute. There is another way to see this." I take a deep breath, shut my eyes, and ask how I can change my perception of the situation based on the present moment. Doing this almost always brings with it some level of empathy, compassion, and understanding, which immediately defuses any negative feelings.

I used to be so preoccupied with my negative self-talk that I could not even see my surroundings accurately. I was always on the verge of crisis mode, and it didn't take much to push me over the edge. Of course, at the time I would never have admitted this, as I was deeply invested in believing that my way of seeing things was the right way. But the truth was that when

I looked to the past to determine how I should react, I saw things in the distorted mirror of addiction. Similarly, when I worried about the future, I could not see all of the opportunities that were available, I only saw negative outcomes.

Perhaps it is an oversimplification, but people basically have two experiences in life. Some go through life grumbling and angry, complaining and unhappy. Other people seem to take things in stride, be more able to shake negative things off, and be happy in the moment. I decided I wanted to choose the latter. I began to look at myself in a different way when in upsetting situations. I saw that the only difference between peace of mind and conflict was the lens through which I viewed the situation, and the choice of lens was entirely up to me. I am continuing to learn to choose peace of mind by being in the present moment. By learning to accept things I can't change, and allowing people to be how they choose to be, I consistently find peace of mind.

Peak Performance and the Present Moment

Throughout my career, and in many of my personal pursuits, I have been interested in peak performance and positive psychology. I am fascinated by what facilitates the highest levels of human functioning, even the miraculous, and allows some people to overcome obstacles that would stop others in their tracks. Over three decades of study, I have observed one extremely important thread of truth common to all optimal levels of performance, be it in athletics, relationships, or work:

> When we are unwavering in our focus on the present, we open the door to opportunities and possibilities rather than obstacles and excuses. We move, think, and perform at higher levels than when we are preoccupied with negative thoughts or images of the past or future. This is the land where healing occurs and opportunity is realized.

To achieve this takes more than just words. There are numerous books on "the now," many of them very good. Rather than simply repeat what some of them say, in this book I present stories to illustrate and inspire, as well as practical exercises and lessons to both grasp and apply these ideas to your life. Let's start with a story.

A friend of mine, Dr. Curt Erikson, is a sports psychologist who works with Olympic and other elite athletes. When Curt interviewed Tiger Woods at the AT&T Golf Tournament in 2000, Woods confirmed that, "Focus in the moment is THE most important aspect of my game." Of course, this is often easier said than done, so let us look more closely at how to develop this skill through real life experience.

Curt has had much adventure in his life, including a climb up Mt. Everest. Curt shared with me the following account of his experience:

"I had an opportunity to be involved as a sports scientist on a group climb in the Himalayas. While camped atop a glacier we were forced to deal with nearly constant avalanches. Every hour a potentially deadly avalanche crashed down the mountain. At first, there was the temptation to become preoccupied with worrying about the next avalanche. But to worry could kill us, because, combined with the constant stress of altitude sickness, worrying would leave us with no energy for doing what we needed to do. The key to our survival became being focused on exactly what we were doing at the moment we were doing it. Our situation demanded that we stay in the moment. One of the Sherpas said, 'The tiger of the mind is more dangerous than the real tiger.' If I focused on the next day, or the previous day, I would be robbed of the necessary energy to keep going. To look to the past or the future would take away from my concentration and alertness, and would make my mind too tired and preoccupied to face any new dangers. I began practicing a climbing mantra, 'Two steps forward. Stop and breathe.'

"The evenings and nights were the most difficult times. Our exhausted minds wanted to wander yet we needed to remain alert and attentive to a variety of tasks. In the long hours of darkness we all struggled with our demons, those little chatterboxes of worry that would have destroyed our ability to concentrate. If I had allowed myself to drift from the 'now' I would have placed myself and the others in the group in great danger. We became a team dedicated to being in the present moment. We monitored each other and helped each other stay focused. Staying in the moment was, in a very real sense, a matter of survival. By staying oriented in the present we grew closer, and we all came down the mountain safely."

When I gave the above story to Curt to read for accuracy, he put a note in the margin that perfectly summarizes the key to peak performance: Focusing in the moment puts the person into the picture of possibilities.

Within Curt's story are the Six Key Principles to Peak Performance that are directly applicable to healing the Addictive Personality and creating peak performance in your life. Below, worded in language similar to Curt's story, are the principles that not only help in healing the Addictive Personality but also bring opportunity and success into your life.

Six Principles to Peak Performance and Realized Opportunity

1. **Stay focused.** When there are "avalanches" of problems in your life, rather than giving in to the temptation to become preoccupied with worrying about the last or the next problem, stay focused on what is happening right now.

2. **See beyond worry.** Know that worrying can leave you with no energy for doing what you need to do. The key to your success is not to be consumed by worry, but to see beyond it, to the horizon of possibilities. With your mind unencumbered with worry you can focus on exactly what you are doing when you are doing it.

3. **Treat every situation with the same dedication.** No matter how menial, enjoyable, or frightening you may find a task, see every situation as demanding that you stay in the moment.

4. **Don't get robbed.** If out of fear you stay focused on tomorrow, or yesterday, you will be robbed of the necessary energy to create the life you want today. Watch for energy drainers and time robbers.

5. **Know what distracts you from greatness.** Dwelling on the past or the future takes you away from the concentration, mindfulness, and alertness you need to face new challenges and opportunities. Ask yourself, "How do I sabotage my greatness?"

6. **Create a team.** In your daily activities, if you allow yourself to drift from the "now" you place yourself, and the other people around you, in a less than an optimal situation. Be it with your family, friends, or co-workers, decide to become a team dedicated to the present moment. Support and remind each other. By staying in the present, you all grow closer.

I wish I could tell you that knowing and practicing these principles is all you need to heal and be successful, but knowing these principles is only half the task. Knowing the patterns and strategies your Addictive Personality will come up with to keep you under its control and away from the Truth-Based Personality is the other half. Your Addictive Personality is already busy strategizing on how to ignore this book. As I have said many times already, the Addictive Personality is not going to go down without a fight, and it is in your best interest to know all of its tricks and strategies for distraction. Remember, there is no greater limit that you can place upon yourself than addictive thoughts. The following are the Six Strategies of the Addictive Personality that, if gone unnoticed, keep you from implementing the Six Principles of Peak Performance and Realized Opportunity. When you think these thoughts, a negative image is produced in your mind. To help break out of the negative patterns, each strategy is followed in bold face by the positive alternative of the Truth-Based Personality.

Six Old Patterns of the Addictive Personality and Six Truth-Based Alternatives

1. I can't: I can't possibly do this. Nobody has ever before done this.
   I can: I will throw a lifeline into mastery and pull myself toward it.

2. I failed: I failed before at this.
   I learn: I am empowered with learning from every experience.

3. I suck: I have always been bad at this.
   I do my best: I take joy in learning new skills and don't have to be perfect.

4. They said: [Name] always said that I would never be able to do this.
   I say: I direct my mind to what I say is possible for me.

5. I will be judged by: People are looking over my shoulder.
   I will be supported by: I surround myself with people who believe in me.

6. I'm doomed: If I make a mistake, it will ruin my whole life.
   I am free: If I make a mistake I will learn and grow from it.

A number of techniques can help you overcome these old patterns and more easily adopt the principles for peak performance. All of these techniques include some form of relaxing and refocusing your mind, as well as utilizing the breath in some way.

Watching the Breath

An effective way of becoming focused in the present is to use a simple technique that can be easily practiced, even in times of distress. This technique works best if you are able to close your eyes, though it can certainly be done with your eyes open. Simply bring your attention to your breath: the inflow and the outflow. Begin to watch the rise and fall of your breath, almost as if you were at the beach watching waves come in and out. If your attention wanders at first, gently remind yourself of your task and refocus on the breath. Though your breathing should be natural and unforced, it is helpful to breathe full, deep breaths, filling the chest and the abdominal area.

Some people attach a phrase or affirmation to the breath. This can be something as simple as silently saying on the inhalation, "I am," and, on the exhalation, "relaxed." You can also use a single word, such as one or now. Experiment to find what works best for you.

The breath has been called the doorway to our inner life. Use of it is certainly a practical and powerful way to let go of your preoccupations with the past and the future. Start out with taking five minutes, three times per day, to practice. Additionally, any time you find yourself in the Addictive Personality, focus on your breath and say, "There is another way to think about this."

How the Truth-Based Personality Uses Acceptance to Create Deep Change and Peace-Centered Relationships

It may come as a surprise to read that using the principles outlined in this book, or any undertaking of self-improvement, can actually become part of the problem rather than the solution. I don't think anybody buys a self-help book if they don't desire positive change; however, the starting point for affecting change is crucial. As counter-intuitive as it may seem now, there is one approach that will make this book a healing journey for you:

In order to truly change, we must first accept ourselves just as we are, without reservation.

Direct your inner gaze beyond your negative image of yourself and toward your essential wholeness. Or, just stop. Then see what is there.

What I discovered was that in order for me to get off the Addictive Personality's treadmill of self-improvement, I didn't need to *do* more, rather, I needed to approach myself with an attitude of acceptance and love. I had to stop finding things wrong with me and beating myself up about them. As long as I beat myself up, positive change was impossible.

When I was on the treadmill of self-improvement, I would first condemn myself, then I'd vow to change. This is how my Addictive Personality kept its hold on me while deluding me into thinking I was doing something positive. The only change that occurred when I condemned myself was that I ended up feeling worse about myself. The result was that I become more deeply entrenched in my addictive behavior. The solution was to stop.

This same phenomenon is true in our relationships with other people. If we judge and condemn them, and then demand that they change, nothing positive is going to happen. Sure, their behavior may alter, and you may feel temporarily in control, but peace and happiness are not attained. It is only a matter of time before a relapse in the addictive behavior occurs. Let's face it, people generally know what they need to change about their lives and they really don't need constant reminders about it. Change is difficult to implement and peace of mind is elusive; otherwise most of us would be happy and addiction free already. The evidence can be seen in the many people who have stopped their previous addictive behavior, but are really not any happier in life after they do.

Recognized Essential Value

So, what is missing in the above approach? In the years I was a practicing psychologist I discovered that I was by far the most helpful when I was able to see the essential value of my client, separate from their behavior, and extend acceptance to them. This idea changed my life when I practiced it throughout my day. If we look to history for people who have really made a difference in the world through service, this is fundamentally how they approached humanity. I call this practice "Recognized Essential Value" (REV). When we practice Recognized Essential Value, in ourselves and others, we are looking beyond behavior, illness, political beliefs, race, sexuality, and so forth, and seeing the essential value of the individual.

With Recognized Essential Value come compassion and acceptance, as well as increased energy and well-being. I often use the acronym for Recognized Essential Value, REV, and remind myself to "REV up my life."

Most people don't wake up one morning and say, "Gee, I think I will go get some therapy," or "Hey, I think I will make a major life change and deal with my addictions." Typically, prior to taking such actions they have already beaten themselves up for many years. They are in dire need of someone who practices Recognized Essential Value to see beyond the behavior. The same is true with people who may be facing challenges not of their own creation. They need recognition of their essential value much more than they need judgment and advice.

Steve came to see me following a separation from his wife. As a construction supervisor, Steve had previously identified strongly with the image he had of himself as a family man. He stated that he was having a hard time adjusting to the separation and that he was often depressed. During the first two months that he was seeing me, he dated several women. He would have a week or two of heavy romance with one woman, then break up with her, and then feel empty and think that nobody could ever replace his wife. He repeated this again and again. Steve began to see that he could come to our sessions and talk openly about what was going on in his life without feeling negatively judged by me. And because I practiced Recognized Essential Value, Steve began to judge himself less harshly, and slowly he opened up.

After several months, Steve was able to share with me that as a child he had been molested by a male relative over a period of years. Finally he revealed his deeply hidden fear that he might be homosexual. Steve had had several homosexual experiences as an adult and felt tremendous guilt as a result.

Eventually, Steve began to explore the issues surrounding his molestation and his questions about his sexuality. During this time my primary task as his therapist was to see beyond what Steve was seeing, and practice Recognized Essential Value, because if Steve could feel accepted despite his own negative self-judgment and guilt, he would be able to explore his issues without being so full of shame.

Most of us have some guilt and shame. Think of ways you can practice Recognized Essential Value in your own daily life. The next time you are tempted to judge someone or yourself, catch yourself and decide instead to practice Recognized Essential Value. The compassion that results can help transform and motivate you to live the life you want.

The Addictive Personality's formula for change:
Judgment, Guilt, and Shame = Motivation to Change

The Truth-Based Personality's formula for change:
Recognized Essential Value = Motivation for Change

To my mind any effective relationship or partnership, be it personal or professional, works not so much because of what is said, but because of practicing Recognized Essential Value, which includes the attitude of acceptance. The attitude of acceptance is, "I accept you as you are today and see the opportunity for growth in you, and should you want to look at various aspects of your life, I am here to support you through it while recognizing your essential value, without judgment." This is what I aspire to practice, professionally, personally, and as a parent.

Here are a few thoughts about the nature of acceptance and how it can heal the Addictive Personality:

- Our energy is exhausted when we judge, analyze, compare, and criticize. On the other hand, we feel enlivened when we extend acceptance.

- Acceptance is based on the present moment. Judgment is based on the past.

- Acceptance does not mean condoning negative behavior. It simply means that to change our own negative behavior (or to encourage another to change), we must see that there is a worthwhile person beneath the behavior.

- Peace of mind comes from accepting things that are not within our power to change. This means recognizing that we cannot control other people.

- Acceptance does not include any expectations. Acceptance is not attached to future outcomes.

- Accept what is and find opportunity. Judge what is and miss opportunity.

Peace of Mind

Forgiveness ⟵——————— Acceptance ——————⟶ Seeing Commonalities

High Self-Esteem

Where judgment makes love conditional,
acceptance allows love to be itself.

Judgment sets criteria for love.
Acceptance sets none.

In judgment we become constricted, rigid, and fearful.
In acceptance we become open, fluid, and free.

Let me suggest an experiment that you can conduct to illustrate for yourself, on a feeling level, the difference between the Truth-Based Personality practice of Recognized Essential Value and the Addictive Personality practice of judgment. Set aside two hours of your day. In the first hour, concern yourself with the past, especially regarding what people have or have not done for you or to you. Be as judgmental as you can, passing judgment on everybody who crosses your mind or your path. Mentally criticize yourself and others mercilessly. Don't act upon your critical thoughts. Just pay attention to how you feel while you are thinking judgmental thoughts. Do you feel good about yourself? Do you feel close to other people? Do you feel at ease and free? Or are you scared and uptight? Are you effective?

During the second hour switch to practicing Recognized Essential Value. Begin with a few minutes of the breathing exercise presented earlier in this chapter. See the innermost truth of love in people, even if it is just a faint flicker deep beneath the surface. If you have a particularly hard time practicing Recognized Essential Value with someone in particular, imagine what kinds of events must have occurred in his or her life that would lead to his or her current behavior; understand how much he or she unconsciously yearns for someone to see essential value. Look beyond the behavior and see the whole person. Imagine that you were born just today, at this hour, that everything is fresh and new. Don't be concerned with what you or other people have or have not done, or are doing right now. Instead, choose to focus on the fact that everybody wants and needs to be loved, accepted, and affirmed for who they are, absent of any blame, punishment, or expectations. Now how do you feel? Ask yourself the same questions as you did for the hour of judgment and note the difference.

By experimenting with an hour of judgment and an hour of Recognized Essential Value, you will learn that you really do choose to develop the personality in which you operate. Whether you extend judgment or practice Recognized Essential Value is a choice that only you can make. And, consciously or unconsciously, it is a choice that you make every minute of every day. With practice, you will find you can just as easily choose one as the other.

Deep Change Versus Surface Change

We are at a point in our discussion where it is of benefit to both summarize and elaborate. Every attempt to heal the Addictive Personality will be met with fierce resistance, thus the need for the subject to be approached from a variety of angles. Understanding the difference between deep and surface change serves this purpose.

> The paradox of change is that we can't effect deep change until we first accept ourselves just as we are.

> People can change the most deeply not through our condemnation, but through our ability to recognize their essential value.

For many years I was afraid, although for much of that time I covered it up so thoroughly I didn't even realize it. The main defense my Addictive Personality used to cover my fear was judgment, which included what I have come to call the Four C's, the belief that constantly *comparing, criticizing, controlling,* and *condemning* are traits that bring security and peace. I created years of suffering until I finally saw that the Truth-Based Personality could obtain happiness, opportunity, and freedom through the act of practicing acceptance.

After many years of clinical practice and training interns, I noticed that certain assumptions I made were rarely questioned, but needed to be when it came to treating the Addictive Personality. For one, there was an assumption that individuals who sought treatment were having some problems in certain areas of their life and that they desired change. I saw myself as an assistant in this goal and would try to help the client become a "higher functioning" person. I slowly realized that with the Addictive Personality, it is not so straightforward. In my own personal growth, for example, for years I had tried many times to "change for the better," only to revert back to my old addictive patterns and the Four C's. A person may say he wants to change, but my claims were followed by a trail of failed attempts thanks to my delusional thinking. It's like tearing down a house because of old, termite-eaten wood and flimsy construction, and then rebuilding with the same damaged materials and unsafe techniques. I came to see there is more than meets the eye in what change is and how we can really achieve it.

After years of failing to find happiness despite changing many things in my life, including stopping addictive behaviors, I came to see that a certain phenomenon must occur before deep change can occur. By "deep change" I mean change on the behavioral, emotional, intellectual, and spiritual levels. I call this phenomenon the paradox of change, and it is an aspect of Recognized Essential Value. When it comes to the Addictive Personality, I find it helpful to think of two different approaches to change: the Power Over Approach, which uses pride and willpower, and the Powerlessness Approach, which uses humility and honesty. The differences in these approaches are as follows.

The Power Over Approach

I grew up with horses and livestock. As a young man working on ranches, I observed many different approaches to working with horses. In those days, the primary method of training was to assert power over the horse by any means in order to have it do what you wanted. "Breaking" the horse had everything to do with overpowering and nothing to do with developing trust and respect. In many ways, this is the same approach the person with an Addictive Personality takes when attempting to change their behavior. Unfortunately, this kind of change is really more a part of the problem than the solution. The Power Over Approach is born from and perpetuates the Addictive Personality's belief that we should be able to control all things through our will and domination.

It is also a good example of what our Addictive Personality does to control the situation when confronted about an addiction. Because we do not want to appear or have to admit to being out of control, we may concede to some level of problem, but we will steadfastly insist on our ability to control it. The next step is usually the defiant use of willpower to prove our point. An example would be to stop drinking for one month to "prove" that we don't have a problem. This kind of change is all based on having the willpower to "just say no" to what we see as the problem or what we want to change, such as alcohol, gambling, or an addictive relationship. If we are successful, even temporarily, the Addictive Personality feels we have proven that we can in fact take control whenever we wish. Thus, our Addictive Personality remains fully intact and largely unquestioned and unexamined.

This pattern describes the way I was for many years. I was always quick to claim victory over my addictions by periodically stopping my addictions. But these small victories were really evidence of an ongoing and progressive downward spiral that led me right back to addiction and suffering. Before I finally got honest with myself, I saw my claims of success as "proof" that I could control my addictive behaviors at will. I told myself "Hey, I can control this, so why not risk going back to a little drug use (or whatever the specific addiction was)."

To heal my Addictive Personality I have to get honest and admit that Power Over Approaches to addiction never fully work.

To heal the Addictive Personality we need to look beyond the behavior. Even if the specific behavior is stopped for good, if the thinking behind the Addictive Personality is never addressed untold suffering continues. Thus, this kind of change is only "surface change," at best.

The Power of Powerlessness Approach

When I was caught in my addictions, I never much liked the phrase "I'm powerless," because I saw it as synonymous with "I'm a weak and ineffective victim." I think this is a primary reason I steered clear of helpful programs and approaches for such a long time. My Addictive Personality let me think I was Superman, and I equated the idea of being powerless with being pathetic and useless. As I began to look more honestly at my life and the way I thought, I realized if deep change and healing were ever going to occur, a new approach was needed. Recognizing that the Power Over Approach had not worked was the first step.

This is actually the first move out of the insanity of the Addictive Personality. When it comes to change, insanity can very simply be defined as when we continue to assert the same approach and expect different results. Our Addictive Personality never wants us to wake up to this simple fact, because it is the beginning of the end of its hold over us.

Paradoxically, I finally could begin anew when through hard honesty, I could admit that I had been defeated by my Addictive Personality. This was the beginning of deep change for me.

Hard Honesty

For most people, honesty is really "honesty light." Practicing "hard honesty" recognizes and evaluates the beliefs that drive the Addictive Personality. Hard honesty not only sees and tells the truth, it *requires* consistency among thoughts, words, and actions. The combination of hard honesty and the Power of Powerlessness leads to deep change and almost always comes from some kind of crisis. And yet, it is from this place that healing and growth will occur. It is where we are able to transcend the Addictive Personality by adopting the new ways of thinking inherent within the Truth-Based Personality.

However, it is useful to recall that the Addictive Personality rarely goes out without a significant fight. The trump card that the Addictive Personality often will resort to is logic. Common sense is actually on the side of the Power Over Approach. It is logical to think that if you want to change something that is out of control, apply an "in-control" approach. Having a somewhat intellectual mind, I fell prey to this argument more than most. When I was finally willing to use hard honesty, however, I saw that this approach simply does not work. To begin using some hard honesty, ask yourself the following questions:

- Why is it that so many people in addictive relationships stay in them, or repeat them after splitting up?
- Why is it that people who are abused so often continue being abused or become perpetrators?

- Why is it that people who grow up with an alcoholic parent so often marry one, or become one themselves?
- Why is it that even when one knows the dangers and suffering caused by certain behaviors, they do them anyway?

Logic and common sense tell us that a person with even half a brain would not do such things. Yet, as you can see, when it comes to the Addictive Personality, logic and common sense simply don't apply, no matter how smart we are. In fact, sometimes it is the smartest people who are the most deeply ensnared within the Addictive Personality.

Healing the Addictive Personality can seem paradoxical. Instead of continuing to exert greater willpower in an endless pattern of behavior to prove your ability to control, try using hard honesty in the Power of Powerlessness Approach. You will begin to see that when you are in the grip of the Addictive Personality your life is out of hand and full of suffering, not to mention the pain we have caused others. To get to this place requires a major shift in thinking and how we see ourselves, and it is not for the timid or uncommitted. The greatest shift I had to make was moving from a stance of false pride to a more humble view of myself. I can tell you firsthand it is not a stroll in the park to move from the pride of the Addictive Personality to the humility of the Truth-Based personality. Hitting rock bottom is often needed to make such a profound shift.

Hitting Bottom

One of the Addictive Personality's mottos could easily be "I can." I approached my life from a stance of "I can control this," "I can change this," "I can make this happen." These statements sound very positive, but for me they were the grease that kept the wheels of my addicted thought system turning. These seemingly positive thoughts were actually reflective of my fear of powerlessness; I said "I can" because I was afraid to say "I am powerless." The "successes" of the Addictive Personality lead only to a perpetuation of increases in addictive behavior, and the motto of "I can" stays paramount.

Like most people with an Addictive Personality, I kept the vicious cycle moving until I finally saw through it after I hit bottom and employed some very hard honesty. Though I am grateful now for those events that brought me to such a low place, when I hit bottom I didn't say "Oh, thank you for this opportunity to honestly look at my Addictive Personality." In reality, it felt a lot more like loss and pain than progress or positive change. Yet, I knew if I stayed with it, the paradox of the Power of Powerlessness would find me. What helped me to grow and heal was the realization that the pain that resulted from continuing to listen to my Addictive Personality was greater than the pain that would accompany a fundamental shift in my thinking and approach to my life.

I could tell you the horror stories of my personal nadir, but I won't. It is too tempting for my Addictive Personality to engage in comparison to keep itself alive. It would be easy for your Addictive Personality to listen to my story and say, "Oh man, I am nowhere near that bad, there's no need for me to stop" or, on the other side of the spectrum, to say "I am much worse than he was, so I must be hopeless." Suffice it to say that when I hit bottom it turned my world upside down; it was actually a gift. It was a gift that offered me an opportunity to change how I saw myself and to end my continual and useless suffering. That said, I must confess that some of us, myself included, are remedial learners when it comes to healing our Addictive Personalities. To the dismay of those around us, it may take reaching several low points before we make the shift away from the fear-based approach of the Addictive Personality.

How the Truth–Based Personality Creates Opportunity and Miracles

You don't need a "just think positively and abundance will be yours" approach, and this is not what I offer. What I do promise is that with the practice of hard honesty, Recognized Essential Value, the Power of Powerlessness, and relaxation breathing techniques we can create moments in our lives where we feel complete and fulfilled, moments with no perception of lack, only wholeness, happiness, and new opportunity. Though initially such moments may be fleeting, they will be enough to begin to spontaneously break through the confines of the Addictive Personality's beliefs and patterns. With this we begin to become aware of all that's available to us at all times, which I refer to as recognized opportunity. We can increase the frequency and duration of these spontaneous breakthroughs by being absolutely clear about what it is that we want.

> Above all else, peace of mind is what I want.
> This very moment I want to recognize my essential value,
> which is unmarred by my actions.
> How could I not receive what I want
> when I ask for what I already have?

Several years ago I was diagnosed with double bacterial pneumonia that could not be brought under control. This was the third time in my adult life I faced a severe physical challenge (the first was the autoimmune disease that took my hearing, the second was a prostate condition). Also, there was concern among my doctors that the illness could affect my brain. I felt that, despite being conscientious about my diet and exercise, I was locked unfairly into a life of ill health, and I was desolate at the thought of facing another possible disability or even death. It was a misty winter day, and I was running a high fever. A specialist had been called, and the situation wasn't looking too promising. Somewhere in the span of a few weeks, an unusual thought broke through my delirium: see beyond your body, beyond the illness, and see the purpose. I still had a lot of tubes stuck in me, I was on oxygen, and I had a 105-degree fever, but something changed. In the end, I was grateful for what occurred. My purpose was to learn to receive more love from those who cared for me the most. A healing awareness came over me as I realized what I was there to learn. There was nothing that I had to do in that moment other than be exactly where I was, experiencing exactly what I was experiencing. It was miraculous.

> A miracle is a shift in our perception in a way that transforms the thought or belief that a moment ago was causing us pain, into a thought or belief that brings us peace of mind and gratitude.

Whereas defenses always bring what they were meant to guard against, miracles always bring with them the awareness of new opportunity. My suggestion to you: believe in them.

In contrast, the Addictive Personality is concerned with getting what it believes will bring happiness, which is always something that has a form. By form I mean the Addictive Personality dictates that our happiness depends on *getting* more and that the way to get more is by *doing* more. The Addictive Personality keeps us believing that what we have is never enough. Once we have what we think we need, then our energy goes into guarding it, and getting more.

The Addictive Personality believes that abundance is defined by material wealth, "perfect" relationships, and elevated status. It fears that once you get these things, you might lose them. It convinces you that if you give away anything you value, you will have less of it. This "false abundance," sadly, is the position from which our culture operates, and it fosters and fuels the addictive lifestyle. In contrast, the Truth-Based Personality sees "true abundance" as the simple recognition that what is of value does not decrease in value over time, and does not need to be guarded. What is of true value grows when it is given away. When we embrace abundance from the perspective of the Truth-Based Personality, we determine what is valuable in a completely different way than when we view the world through the lens of the Addictive Personality, where abundance is really only a disguised belief of scarcity.

You may have noticed that most approaches to change, be they religious, spiritual, psychological, or political, address our values system. The problem is, and this is often overlooked even by experts, many of our values systems still employ the Addictive Personality's tactics. Since all of this can be kind of confusing at first, the following are practical ways to sort out what is of true value and leads to true opportunity and abundance.

Creating Opportunity and Abundance: What Is Valuable and What Is Not

- The true test is whether something increases when it is given away. For example, Recognized Essential Value, love, kindness, compassion, and caring all increase when shared with others.

- Time does not diminish what is of value.

- The Addictive Personality says, "I must do something else before I can feel self-worth and experience peace." The Truth-Based Personality says, "In a quiet mind, peace and self-worth become known."

- What is of value needs no defense.

- What you value is what you choose to value. Love is drawn to itself. Attack is drawn to itself. The choice you make of what you draw to yourself is entirely up to you.

- A key to healing is to give to others what you already have, instead of trying to get what you think you need.

- True abundance and opportunity offer escape from the thought that you are not enough through Recognized Essential Value.

- True abundance and opportunity see no value in fear, because true abundance recognizes that there is nothing of value that can be lost.

- When you know that you have love within, what else would you want to do but share what you have?

- True abundance values win/win situations. False abundance values win/lose situations.

The Myth about True Abundance

I had the good fortune to spend time in India with one of the great teachers of our time: Mother Teresa. Whenever she started up a mission she never thought in terms of scarcity, saying, "Oh, we can't do this because there is not enough money." Mother Teresa knew that love and kindness were all that were truly important. Although she did not use these words, throughout my stay with her I witnessed her practicing Recognized Essential Value time and time again. When she cared for a dying man, she saw beyond his frail body to the essential value of his soul shining within. When she fed a starving child, she saw beyond the hungry reaching hands to the essential value in those grateful young eyes. Her example demonstrates that when you choose to see the essential value in another living being, you can no longer ignore them. When you stop ignoring and start loving, healing can begin.

The Addictive Personality sees obstacles and calculates
loss in every situation.
The Truth-Based Personality sees opportunities to learn,
give, and receive in every situation.

The Addictive Personality clings to fear in the irrational
belief that it offers protection.
The Truth-Based Personality sees beyond fear, knowing that fear
does not offer protection, rather that fear attracts what it fears.

The Addictive Personality clings to the negative past in the belief
that grudges and guilt are useful.
The Truth-Based Personality finds healing in seeing the essential
value in the present and letting go of the past.

The Addictive Personality uses scarcity, blame, and unworthiness
to deflect responsibility from thoughts, words, and actions.
The Truth-Based Personality embraces responsibility through the
practice of Recognized Essential Value.

The Addictive Personality equates judgment with healing.
The Truth-Based Personality equates loving with healing.
The Addictive Personality tells us we are upset because the situation
is not how we think it should be or because something might
happen that we can't control.
The Truth-Based Personality tells us we are upset because of how we
perceive the situation and that the most powerful healing
forces are forgiving thoughts.

The Thirteen Core Beliefs of the Truth–Based Personality

As we have seen, the Truth-Based Personality is built upon love, the present moment, acceptance, and abundance. The beliefs of the Truth-Based Personality bring healing and happiness through the following core beliefs.

Truth–Based Belief Number One:
What I see in others reflects my own state of mind. I lack nothing to be happy, grateful, and effective right now. There is an underlying unity to all life.

The first sentence affirms that "truth" is a reaction to our own state of mind projected outward. This is no easy concept to grasp because to do so means we admit we are ultimately responsible for our reactions and how we see things. We are always looking through the filter of our own thoughts and beliefs, which determines how we see other people and situations. I have been practicing this truth for three decades now, and I still can have resistance to it. It is always much easier to fall into the Addictive Personality's game plan where we constantly blame others, seeing a world that is against us. The Truth-Based Personality has no beliefs that support the blame game, and instead sees each and every situation as an opportunity for growth and learning. Once I practiced hard honesty with myself I saw that it has been habitual for me to be a "blaming victim" rather than a "responsible creator." This habit continued for the simple reason that it was easier than positive change.

The rest of the belief recognizes that we are not detached from each other, but are, in fact, connected by the thread of love. It would be hard to imagine a more isolating existence than being a prisoner of war in solitary confinement; some lose their will to live, some lose their sanity. Yet others survive the experience mentally and emotionally intact. Accounts from survivors suggest that they have one thing in common: They were able to realize that, despite their solitude, they were not alone. Some thought about their families and sent them love; some felt the love their families sent to them. They did not see the confines of a prison cell as able to keep love from them. They survived by understanding that love knows no boundaries.

Some survivors connected mentally with the other inmates. They sent silent messages of strength and compassion and understood that others were doing the same for them. They could feel the strength of their fellow prisoners lifting them above the despair. Still others survived their ordeal through a deepening relationship with a power greater than themselves.

It is my belief that those who developed severe emotional problems and lost all sense of purpose and hope believed they were completely alone when the cell door closed. The experiences of the survivors show us that the strength of the human spirit lies in the knowledge that we are all intimately and deeply connected. Love never abandons us. It is we who sometimes choose to abandon love.

Truth–Based Belief Number Two:
My safety lies in my defenselessness. Because love needs no defense, acceptance brings peace of mind.

For years my Addictive Personality told me that my defenses (anger and guilt) would make me feel secure, yet all that resulted were increased feelings of isolation and fear. I finally realized it would be impossible to feel secure as long as I continued to build walls to hide behind. A simple truth that has not been easy for me to fully grasp is:

Safety, success, and security are by-products of love, not of fear.

I decided that if this were true, and if I wanted safety, success, and security, then I had to stop listening to the fear preached by my Addictive Personality. Inevitably, my experiences in the world changed as I stopped trying to change what was outside of myself and instead focused on changing my thoughts. This in turn nurtured my ability to trust in the powers of compassion and love.

WE CEASE

Trust is a state of joy and acceptance of what is.

It is where we find freedom and healing through giving.

We cease trying to always do more
because all is done.

We cease trying to control and manipulate
because all is as it is for us to learn.

We cease trying to aspire to be someplace else
because we choose to be fully here now.

We cease trying to change other people
because we see the truth of who they are.

We cease being fearful
because we know love.

When we act defensively we just feel more insecure, afraid, and distant from those we're trying to be close to. In all my relationships, whether professional, familial, romantic, or friendship, I have found that becoming less defensive and more communicative results in increased closeness and allows me to be far more trusting, effective, and genuine.

In my close relationships, acknowledging and talking about my fears, instead of trying to defend myself against them, has led me to feel safer and allowed me to know the other person better.

Truth–Based Belief Number Three:
Love is unconditional. My self–worth is not based upon measuring up to some external standard.

When I was a child I learned that when I behaved according to the wishes of someone else, such as my parents or teachers, I received praise. When I didn't, I was ignored or punished. In families like mine, where appearances were extremely important, children grow up feeling that anything short of perfection is failure. I spent years vacillating between working hard and giving up, because even attaining a high goal meant, at the most, only momentary satisfaction. I learned that no matter what I did, or how well I did it, it was never quite enough.

> When we believe that our self-worth is based upon our behaving
> according to some external standard or level of performance,
> we invariably end up with feelings of inadequacy,
> regardless of how well we do something.

Most parents want the best for their children, but we need to be careful about the messages we give them. Today's culture puts enormous expectations and unnecessary stress on kids. As I write this, my oldest daughter is studying for the SAT. I remind her often to do her best, but I also remind her that the test is only about a number and the game of college admission and not about her worth as a person.

In contrast, Kathy, a former client, grew up in a family where perfect performance and behavior were the best way to get positive attention from her mother. If Kathy received five A's and one B+, her mother would ask, "Why didn't you get straight A's? You want to get into Stanford, don't you?" Later, Kathy did, in fact, go to Stanford on a number of academic scholarships. Despite her "success" she often woke up with her stomach in such a knot that she had to vomit. She feared receiving any grade less than an A. As an adult, Kathy kept up her pattern of overachieving and perfectionism and became an executive and part owner in a large computer company at the age of twenty-seven, making millions of dollars. But Kathy was still plagued by a relentless fear of failure.

Andy grew up in a family similar to Kathy's, but he adopted a different way of compensating for his feelings of inadequacy. Andy did poorly in school, never went to college, and ended up in a menial job. He never put out much effort despite the fact that he was very bright. From an early age, because of his parents' constant "encouragement" and dissatisfaction, Andy adopted the attitude of "No matter what I do, it's not going to be good enough, so why bother? If I never try, I'll never fail."

I combined both ways of being in the world: Because I believed my self-worth was based on an external standard, I see-sawed between periods of academic and athletic accomplishment and periods of apathy and drug use. Though not always apparent from the outside, inside I felt I was either a star or a loser, depending on which end of the arc the pendulum of my low self-esteem had swung. Although one is more culturally acceptable than the other, either position kept me feeling fearful and worthless.

The common thread between Kathy, Andy, and myself was the belief of the Addictive Personality in each of us, namely, that our performances and behaviors determined our worth as human beings. The task in healing was for us to let go of this addictive belief. To end the addictive cycle of behavior we needed to recognize that the love we deserve and our self-worth are not based on meeting external standards.

> We were all born into this world
> fully worthwhile, lovable, and without shame.
> It is our task in healing, individually and collectively,
> to get back in touch with this core of who we are.

Truth–Based Belief Number Four:
Forgiveness, with hard honesty, ensures peace.

Albert Einstein once suggested that if humankind was to survive the nuclear age our thinking would have to change. He knew that the most powerful forces are not external, but are actually our own minds.

Defense and attack are the Addictive Personality's way of thinking. If we want safety and peace, be it on an interpersonal or a global level, we must change our way of thinking by practicing forgiveness, rather than attack and defense. Initiating forgiveness requires taking responsibility for our thoughts and actions. The first step is to see how forgiveness is often misunderstood. Forgiveness is the shift in our perception that allows us to see our commonalities in the present moment instead of focusing on our differences from the past. Put another way, lack of forgiveness is being entrenched in seeing how we have done, or been done wrong, believing steadfastly that we are right and refusing to see any common ground. The Addictive Personality tells us that withholding forgiveness will keep us safe, but in reality it is like swallowing poison and expecting the *other* person to keel over.

The following text has been adapted from my book *Smile for No Good Reason* (Hampton Roads Publishing, 2000).

Forgiveness Practice Session

Yesterday morning, I found myself with my foot in the kitchen trashcan, trying to stuff in just one more old milk carton, rather than making the trip out to the garbage can. After getting last night's leftovers all over my shoes, I thought the two-minute walk to take out the garbage would have been much easier.

Similarly, this stuffing process is what the Addictive Personality does best. I can let negative or old thoughts directed at myself and others pile up, and not take the time to let go of them. If I keep stuffing without letting go, something sticky and smelly (like anger, envy, revenge, or jealousy) usually ends up on my shoes. Then I have a mess to clean up. The few minutes a day it takes to practice forgiveness makes for a much easier life. Forgiveness is akin to taking out the trash, and for maximum benefit, do it regularly.

I have found in my life that forgiveness practice sessions greatly help to keep my mind clear of thoughts that don't bring me peace. I suggest that once a day, beginning today, schedule five-minute forgiveness sessions. During this time your task is to think about the people in your life, including yourself, and to see beyond their behavior and into who they really are. Imagine their (or your) behavior is like whitecaps on the surface of the ocean. Look beyond the weather and the waves, and into the depths of the water. Visualize a glimmer of light in their hearts, a gentle or invisible smile (which even they may be unaware of). Do the same with yourself. During each session let this light grow brighter, and your smile grow wider.

Undertaking this practice will make you remarkably lighter and happier. People around you will notice the difference too.

Remember, forgiveness does *not* mean that you condone all behaviors, or stop holding others accountable for their actions.

Forgiveness *does* mean that you are willing to look beyond behavior for the essential value in everybody, including yourself.

Forgiveness is a result of seeing yourself and other people in the present moment, not in the past.
Forgiveness is the foundation for healing, happiness, and new opportunity.

Also remember, forgiveness can be misunderstood. The Addictive Personality may come up with many reasons not to forgive. Or it may tell you that forgiveness is judging someone from a position of superiority and then telling them you "forgive" them. Denial and misrepresentation of forgiveness are what the Addictive Personality does best, and it is a habit many of us are entrenched in. Choose not to listen to the unforgiving voice of the Addictive Personality and instead remember:

When you forgive someone, you see the essential value that is within that person, no matter how well hidden it may be by their unbecoming behavior.

Ask yourself honestly: when has staying angry and engaging in defense and attack ever brought me lasting peace of mind or true opportunity?

If you want peace of mind and endless new opportunities, begin to see the value in forgiveness.

Truth–Based Belief Number Five:
Only the present is real. The past is over and the future is not yet here.

Embracing this single thought opens the door to opportunity and happiness while closing the door to fear and worry.

Like so many others, I have lived much of my life worrying about the future. I used to wake up in the morning worrying about the day ahead. I would go to sleep worrying that tomorrow might be even worse. Throughout the day I would critique my performance and wonder what I could have done differently.

I have seen this pattern of worry-critique-worry in many participants in my workshops. Most people have had the experience of having to speak in a group, and few find it a relaxing experience. I often ask the participants to introduce themselves, say a little about their personal interests in the workshop, and add anything else they wish. I have noticed that the closer an individual comes to his or her turn the less he or she listens to what is being said by the current speaker. Instead, they are busy mentally rehearsing what they are going to say. After they get their turn, they're still not fully attentive because they're too busy critiquing and comparing their performance to the others. After the introductions are over, their attention may turn to worrying about whether they'll need to speak again. With all of this distracting mental activity, there's little time left to pay attention to what is really happening in the present moment.

In every day life, it's so easy to fall into this habitual way of thinking and end up missing much of what is going on in our lives. Once again, opportunities are missed thanks to the addictive cycle of worrying, judging, and rehearsing.

> Have you ever missed a turn while driving because you were preoccupied? Think of how many opportunities you miss because you are preoccupied with something that has already happened or worried about something that hasn't yet happened and may never happen at all.

The solution is to consciously bring our focus back to the here-and-now, which is, ironically, both simple to institute yet difficult to maintain. In my workshops I now direct people to be consciously present, listen, and be aware of their minds' habitual need to go into the worry-critique-worry process.

Truth–Based Belief Number Six:
To change my experience, I must first change my thoughts.

In the Truth-Based Personality we direct our minds to pay attention to our thoughts and attitudes rather than wasting our time complaining, judging, finding fault, and being afraid. The key phrase here is "we direct our mind," because we are choosing to see that if we are not happy, we should look first to our own thoughts, rather than habitually blaming, worrying, and judging.

Every situation that arises gives us the opportunity to decide where to direct our mind. These choices never end as long as we are alive. Redirecting your mind toward peace should not be thought of as avoiding challenging situations. To the contrary, this practice allows us to be most effective in every encounter we have. I call this "Peaceful Persistence." Think of how someone like the Dalai Lama or Mother Teresa would approach your latest challenge. I think of Peaceful Persistence as the "Buddhist squeaky wheel," where we make ourselves heard, but from a place of compassion. Currently, I am learning to practice this again. Recently, part of my home was severely flooded. The insurance company did not act in a way that I would term honest: initially they denied my claim. I found myself lying awake at night with my mind seething with angry thoughts and feelings of helplessness. I knew that I could invent elaborate ways to avoid seeing that the source of my upset was my own mind. This is a form of the blame game, an effective strategy for placing responsibility on others and escalating their guilt. In contrast, the Truth-Based Personality sees the anger-blame-guilt pattern for what it is: a condition in which the Addictive Personality convinces us that someone else has done something to upset us, and they should be punished for it. The peaceful alternative to this insanity is adopting a state of mind that recognizes that we often don't perceive what is in our own best interests. Once I realized that my Addictive Personality wanted to punish the insurance company (an impossible task), I was able to take care of the situation with peaceful persistence. Interestingly, the insurance adjusters responded more positively than when I was angry and confrontive.

Truth–Based Belief Number Seven:
Mistakes call for correction and learning.
Judgment and punishment are not needed for growth.

I have always been an introverted and sensitive person, which has made my life a bit of a roller-coaster ride. As an adult I have used this to become more intuitive and feeling with people, but when I was a child I did not really know how to use this to my benefit. I often found myself feeling as though any time I made even the smallest of mistakes I had just let the whole world down. As a teenager I can't recall my parents ever praising me. In fact, it seemed that they were always looking to find fault with me when they weren't preoccupied with their own lives. I felt there must be something wrong with me.

As I grew up, I continued to judge myself harshly when I made mistakes of any kind. When my wife told me she wanted a divorce, I remember thinking, "How can this be? We have the perfect marriage." It took time for me to see that not only did we not have the perfect marriage, but I had behaved in ways I thought I never would, including being covertly critical of my wife. When I acknowledged the mistakes, I came down hard on myself. I was convinced I would never deserve another good relationship. Internally, I had become my own critical parent. As long as I continued to punish myself I stayed stuck in shame, which, of course, made it impossible to have a healthy relationship, and so my belief was proved right.

Very slowly, over a very long period of time, I was able to see that the end of my marriage was an opportunity for learning, not punishment, and I began to explore the fears that had contributed to its collapse. I came to accept responsibility for what I had done without the need to punish myself. Punishment had kept me shackled to the past, but by practicing Recognized Essential Value and forgiveness I was able to move on.

The greatest limit to my learning
is my self-judgment, the playing of old tapes,
and endless punishment.

My mind is limitless in its ability to learn
once I cease to beat myself up.

Creative power, solutions, and opportunities are set free
when I release myself from the confines of self-criticism.

Truth-Based Belief Number Eight:
Only love is real. And what is real cannot be threatened.

Consider the following:
Only your essential value is real.
And your essential value is love.
What is real cannot be threatened.

In the Addictive Personality we always feel threatened. It is impossible to feel threatened and have an optimally functioning and peaceful mind at the same time. The Truth-Based Personality recognizes that the Addictive Personality exists in a world of illusion based upon faulty beliefs. Recognized Essential Value, which is really the practice of unconditional love, has no enemies, no fear of being destroyed: it is everywhere and all that is. There is nothing to oppose what is truly of value, and thus, there is no need for defense.

Truth-Based Belief Number Nine:
I am responsible for my life. Because I choose the feelings that I experience, through my intention I decide upon the goal I would achieve.

With this belief we give up arguing with and blaming others, and we decide to take responsibility for our own lives. When we have peace of mind as our single goal, that is what we will achieve. When we have many conflicting goals, such as wanting to prove other people wrong and be happy, conflict is what we get.

We only need to ask a few questions of people, or watch a few minutes of a political debate, to see how each person sees the world through his or her own filter, coming to different conclusions from the same information.

If we look through green glasses we see a green world; if we look through rose glasses we see a pink-tinted world. Seeing the world through the Addictive Personality we see a world that calls for us to be angry, envious, guilty, and ashamed, and to defend and attack. Seeing the world through the Truth-Based Personality we see a world that calls for us to practice Recognizing Essential Value and to extend love, strive to understand, empathize, and offer compassionate action. We see two different worlds and have two different sets of experience depending upon which personality we choose to develop.

Your intentions are very important, and they actually create outcomes. To clarify your intentions in any situation it can be helpful to ask yourself these questions:

> What do I want to come of this?
> and
> What is the purpose of this situation?

The Addictive Personality will answer these questions very differently from the Truth-Based Personality. It's your life, you choose. Remember, the Addictive Personality will likely tell you that you are someone who needs defenses and will always complain and blame when something is over, whereas the Truth-Based Personality will tell you that you are someone who can create experiences and give to the world, and will direct you to put your intentions at the beginning. Also, when answering these questions of intention, do not focus so much on external events or outcomes. In other words, how do you want to be, respond, and grow, and why?

Many times we are not living the life we want simply because we do not adequately clarify our intention (to learn about some aspect of love) at the outset of a situation, or throughout the day. When we do not clarify our intention we are inviting the Addictive Personality to run wild, creating havoc and continuous dust clouds of conflict in our lives. If you find yourself complaining a lot, or if you often feel like a victim, you may want to start a practice of asking these two questions of intention.

Truth–Based Belief Number Ten:
I receive what I want by giving what I have.
This cycle of abundance has no limits
and cannot be contained by circumstances.

By viewing the world through the lens of the Addictive Personality, a limited world with little to offer, we scratch and claw for whatever scraps we can whenever we can find them, often regardless of the means. Further, we believe that for us to win others must lose, because that is how the law of scarcity operates.

There is a growing body of research from the fields of psychology, physiology, and economics that is trying to determine what brings lasting success and peak performance. On the basis of this research, my friends and colleagues, Don Goewey and Bonny Meyer, have developed a corporate program called ProAttitude. They found that a "dynamic peace of mind" is at the highest level of functioning. Dynamic peace of mind is a stress-free, highly responsive internal state that we can learn to re-create at any time or in any situation. Goewey and Meyer's findings also suggest that the most effective way to increase what we want is through giving back, whether to our families, our communities, or to the planet itself. "Fearless Self-Confidence" (a term coined by ProAttitude) is what puts us at our absolute best, a state of being that stress cannot unsettle. This essential attitude is what makes us larger than any circumstances. The equation is simple:

To have peace, give peace.
To create opportunity, offer opportunity.
To increase what you want, give what you have.

I call this "centered giving." It is giving from a place of knowing that we are whole and complete, and wanting to share with others. This is in contrast with the Addictive Personality's view of giving, which is motivated by the need to manipulate and control. In the Truth-Based Personality there is no concept of losing. True opportunity is not selective; it does not withhold from some and not from others.

Truth–Based Belief Number Eleven:
I am complete right now.

Your Addictive Personality does not want you to know that you are whole and complete right now, because when you know this your addictive pursuits will stop. When you realize you already have what you're looking for, you will not only feel relief, but also amusement, not dissimilar to looking for your sunglasses and realizing you are already wearing them.

At the time I first stopped using drugs and alcohol, I was searching for answers to some of life's big questions. I meditated regularly, read hundreds of books, studied with spiritual teachers, went to therapy, signed up for retreats, and prayed. Although much of this was beneficial to me and gave me periods of peace, in the end I was still searching. I believed there was something or someone "out there" to find. I had to find the something or someone, and then I would be complete.

Searching can be part of the problem.
Stopping can be the solution.

Does this sound familiar? I run all over my house looking for my car keys; I paw through drawers, look under piles of papers on my desk, ask my kids, and work myself into a frenzy. Finally, I reach into a pocket (the same pocket I had looked in before) and find the keys.

When we develop our Truth-Based Personality, we have a similar experience, but on a more profound level: all of a sudden we find that the love and serenity we've been searching for have been available to us all along. We've been so busy looking everywhere else, it doesn't occur to us to become quiet and look within.

Truth-Based Belief Number Twelve:
My self-esteem comes from within.
I love and accept myself as I am today.

Those of us with feelings of low self-worth often try to become "people pleasers," thinking that if we make everyone feel good, or attain approval from others, then we will feel better about ourselves. The problem is that we *never* feel comfortable unless we're trying to please or seeking constant approval.

Because we project our internal state onto the external world, we cannot truly love and accept others without first loving and accepting ourselves. An example of this occurs in parenting. It may surprise you to learn that many abusive parents actually care deeply about their children. But if, say, a mother does not feel good about herself, no matter what she does she will likely not be able to be the mother she wants to be. This can manifest from being emotionally unavailable to being physically abusive, despite her intentions.

It is important to remember that initially stopping the behaviors of the Addictive Personality may lead to feelings of despair. But continue to practice a change in thinking and healing will come.

Truth-Based Belief Number Thirteen:
I can't change others, but I can change how I perceive them.
Therefore, I choose how I want to respond to them.

This statement reveals the power we have as well as the power we don't have. Despite everything, the Addictive Personality can be unrelenting and may continue to do the opposite of what you know will help. When others engage in behavior that we dislike, it is crucial that we recognize that their behavior is motivated by fear. Fear manifests in many different and unbecoming ways, including anger, jealousy, envy, defensiveness, and blame. When you see that someone is fearful, you are free to extend your understanding and compassion. This, of course, is an outrage to the Addictive Personality, which tells us to reassert control, continue to judge, and resolve to try to change other people.

Be careful not to confuse this with thinking that you should be passive or put in harm's way. In the Truth-Based Personality it is perfectly fine to say how we feel, to speak up about cruelty, violence, or oppressive behavior. But, we are also encouraged to see our *primary* task is to Recognize Essential Value within ourselves and in others. Everything else stems from this.

Let us imagine a father and his seven-year-old son. The boy is sent home from school because he picks fights with another child. His behavior is obviously in no one's best interest, but what is the real need of the child? Should Dad discipline the boy because he sees a need to assert parental control? Or would it be more appropriate to perceive his son's behavior as a bid for attention or a call for help? Should Dad's response come from love, compassion, and a desire to understand his son's experience at school? Or should it come from anger, disappointment, and the need to change the unacceptable behavior?

Does responding with love mean that Dad condones his son's aggression? Of course not. In fact, appropriate consequences will be in order if it continues. But, regardless of the consequences, the Truth-Based Personality recognizes the child's fear and responds with love.

If our primary goal is to control others, chances are that the Addictive Personality is controlling us. If our primary goal is to Recognize Essential Value, and to understand and communicate, chances are we're living in the Truth-Based Personality.

The Core Beliefs of the Addictive Personality and the Truth–Based Personality

On the following two pages you will find a side-by-side comparison of the two personalities. Refer to these lists when you find yourself caught in addictive thinking. Identify which of the addictive beliefs you are primarily operating under, then find the corresponding love-based belief on the facing page. This will help you recognize that you *have* choices and that you *can* change your mind.

Beliefs of the Addictive Personality

1. I am separate from everybody else. I am alone in a cruel, harsh, and unforgiving world.

2. If I want security and success, I must judge others and be quick to defend myself.

3. My perceptions are always correct, and my way is the right way. In order to feel good about myself, I need to be perfect all of the time.

4. Attack and defense are my only safety.

5. The past and the future are real and must be worried about.

6. Guilt is inescapable because the past is real.

7. Mistakes require judgment and punishment. They are not an opportunity for correction and learning.

8. Fear is real. Do not question it.

9. Other people and situations are at fault for my feelings.

10. Another's loss is my gain. Success comes from looking out for number one and pitting myself against others.

11. I need something or someone else to complete me.

12. My self-esteem is based on pleasing someone else.

13. I need to control everyone and everything around me.

You may find it helpful to review this list each morning as a way to start the day on the right foot.

Beliefs of the Truth–Based Personality

1. What I see in others is a reflection of my own state of mind. I lack nothing I need to be happy, grateful, and effective right now. There is an underlying unity to all life.

2. My safety lies in my defenselessness. Because love needs no defense, acceptance is what brings me peace of mind.

3. Love is unconditional. My self-worth is not based on measuring up to some external standard.

4. Forgiveness, with hard honesty, ensures peace.

5. Only the present is real. The past is over and the future is not yet here.

6. To change my experience, I must first change my thoughts.

7. Mistakes call for correction and learning. Judgment and punishment are not needed for growth.

8. Only love is real. And what is real cannot be threatened.

9. I am responsible for my life. Because I choose the feelings that I experience, through my intention I decide upon the goal I would achieve.

10. I receive what I want by giving what I have. This endless cycle of abundance has no limits and cannot be contained by circumstances.

11. I am complete right now.

12. My self-esteem comes from within. I love and accept myself as I am today.

13. I can't change others, but I can change how I perceive them. Therefore, I choose how I want to respond to them.

Forgiveness is the ultimate conduit for peace of mind, as so eloquently stated in *A Course in Miracles:*

What could you want that forgiveness cannot give?

Do you want peace?
Forgiveness offers it.

Do you want happiness, a quiet mind,
a certainty of purpose,
and a sense of worth and beauty
that transcends the world?

Do you want care and safety,
and the warmth of sure protection always?

Do you want a quietness that cannot be disturbed,
a gentleness that never can be hurt,
a deep, abiding comfort,
and a rest so perfect it can never be upset?

All this forgiveness offers you.

The Addictive Personality and the Fear of Intimacy

In our culture, many people think of intimacy as another word for sex. The question "Were you intimate?" is used euphemistically, implying a certain meaning without saying so. Though intimacy can be a part of sexuality, it is much more, and certainly is not limited to romantic relationships. True intimacy is about being open, genuine, unguarded, and fully present. And it is this that the Addictive Personality tells us is not such a good idea.

When I first began working in the field of chemical dependency, most counseling was done solely with the chemically dependent person. Friends, family members, and romantic partners were absent. For years I watched these courageous individuals repeatedly fall short of their potential in relationships. I often witnessed their return to alcohol and drug use, or other addictive behaviors when the old feelings of low self-esteem, past guilt, and shame resurfaced and re-launched the individual into old patterns of relating. Many returned to the familiar territory of blame, anger, and attack in order to avoid having to use hard honesty with themselves, often in response to the frustration and pain they experienced in their close relationships. I realized that working with an individual in such isolation was of little lasting use. The fact is, be it with chemical dependency or any other type of addiction, the arena where they are played out, often with devastating results, is relationships. But the good news is that relationships can also be a vehicle for healing.

In my experience, families and other groups of people can heal together. I have written books and designed workshops that are based on this belief. I ran one program for many years that required family members to participate, a requirement that was often met with great resistance. Some relatives cited a belief that "the problem is with the addict" and that "if he just changed his behavior and cleaned up his act, everything would be normal." Unfortunately, "normal" for these families is, at best, fleeting moments of relating well that are mostly mired in resentment, guilt, and fear of relapse. Once I managed to convince the families to join in the progream, the changes were dramatic. Parents, children, siblings, and spouses were able to reveal their secret feelings of isolation, resentment, and despair. What's more they discovered they were not alone but were amazed to discover that their feelings were shared by other members of the group. Over time it has become clear to me that many of the issues we struggle with share a common theme: the fear of intimacy and trust.

The Confusion between Freedom and Imprisonment

I recently saw an advertisement for a product designed to keep your dog in your yard without a fence, and it made me think of the Addictive Personality. The dog wears a collar that emits a beeping sound when she gets close to the perimeter of the yard. As the unexpecting pooch reaches the outermost boundary of the yard, she receives an electric shock. The voltage is not high enough to hurt her, but it does get her attention, and she quickly learns to respect the perimeter. In fact, most dogs stop at the beeping, or even before, not wanting to risk the consequences of going further and getting zapped.

The Addictive Personality uses the past in a very similar way to the canine shock collar. It keeps us afraid of love and confined to the limited area of its core beliefs. Like a wary dog anticipating a shock, the Addictive Personality is hypervigilant to the warning signs of potential pain. Thus we remain confined in the belief that the experience of love we yearn for is too risky. Like the dog that no longer dreams of roaming beyond the invisible boundaries of her yard, over time we lose the awareness of what it is we yearn for. Instead, we remain stuck in a small yard hemmed in by addictive patterns, occasionally gazing longingly through the fence that isn't really there at all.

No one in their right mind would say they don't want freedom from pain and suffering; however, the Addictive Personality routinely blurs the lines between freedom and imprisonment. Perhaps you have heard of prisoners who are incarcerated at an early age, remain locked up for a long period of time, and then are released. Many find freedom to be unfamiliar and difficult to manage, and soon commit another crime in order to return to the familiarity and safety of imprisonment. Those of us who struggle with the Addictive Personality have probably done something very similar. We create a positive situation, such as sobriety or a relationship, and then sabotage it with old patterns in order to return to the comfort of what is familiar.

Through the work of hard honesty, I realize now that the times when I relapsed with drugs I did so because I was like the newly freed prisoner who could not cope with the unfamiliarity of freedom, opting instead for the "freedom" drugs offered me in the short-term, rather than the delayed gratification of working through my discomfort and finding the truth, wisdom, and real freedom.

The fear of intimacy is really the fear of love, and it is endemic in our society today. Many people live in a self-imposed prison and don't even know it. I did. For years I yearned for closeness yet lived in a world where I felt I had to protect myself from others. I was so busy building walls around my heart I did not see I was imprisoning myself behind them.

At some level I longed to remember my wholeness, and yet I looked for new things to acquire and new goals to achieve in order to feel better about myself. From age thirteen to my mid-twenties, I turned to chemical substances. When I used, I felt momentarily free, powerful, and whole. Yet my drug use became a boomerang, compounding my loneliness and despair.

FREEDOM, TRUTH, AND WISDOM

I found ways to forget my loneliness
and in the process forgot who I was.
I called this freedom.

Like clear water
clouded by the turbulence of tides,
fear became my guide
while love seemed to be locked from my heart.
I called this truth.

I covered my fear with layers of armor,
and locked love out,
until I was afraid of love itself.
I called this wisdom.

My shield became "doing well" and "looking good."
Yet how strong could I make an eggshell?
I began to break,
and beyond the pieces scattered across the floor
I found who I was,
and discovered real freedom, truth, and wisdom.

Although I felt that both my parents loved me, I received many mixed messages from them. With my father, now a recovering alcoholic who drank throughout my childhood, I felt that I was either being spoiled with material things, overworked, or unfairly punished. My mother, also an alcoholic, appeared to be as devoted as any mother could possibly be. But in our house things were far from peaceful. My parents fought a great deal, and I tried to deflect the attention away from their unhappiness by inventing different roles for myself within the family. I was not at all comfortable doing this, yet I knew no other way. I hated my loneliness and isolation, but I was also afraid of closeness because it didn't feel safe to trust anyone. So I feigned elaborate physical illnesses in the hope that I could refocus where the spotlight went in our household and thus control an out-of-control environment.

When I was thirteen, I went to my mother's office one day complaining of back pain. From previous experience, I knew that a physical complaint would at least momentarily capture her attention. I don't remember if I was actually in any physical pain, but what followed set the stage for my adolescence. I was taken to the emergency room and given an injection of a powerful narcotic. Within minutes, I felt the first relief I had ever experienced from the secret emotional pain I had kept carefully hidden. The drug gave me a feeling of wholeness for the first time in my young life. I was admitted to the hospital and diagnosed with a progressive disease characterized by the slow deterioration of the edges of the vertebrae due to physical growth. On an x-ray the vertebrae appeared to be eaten away. Metaphorically, this was my psychological state: I felt that I had been emotionally disintegrating since I was a young child.

The problem was I did not have the chronic physical pain that apparently I was supposed to have. So I began to fake the pain in order to get the all-important injections; they were my only relief, an oasis in a desert of misery. As long as I was high, and in the controlled environment of the hospital, I felt I was in control. I was the focus of my family's attention. My command post was my hospital bed; the drugs served as both weapons and armor. At the time, of course, my need to manipulate others was unconscious. Only thirteen years old, I was afraid and confused, and my "illness" seemed to take on a life of its own.

Within a few weeks, my armor got thicker and harder as the first of many full body casts was plastered around me, and about this time I began to wonder if I might be crazy. Although the situation felt strangely safe, I knew it wasn't "normal." In order to feel what I thought was love I would time my narcotic injections to coincide with my family visits. This was the first of dozens of hospitalizations. At one point I even had a hospital bed at home along with the narcotics. I became afraid to leave my room, because it had everything I needed to feel safe: my bed, drugs, body cast, and television. From the self-imposed imprisonment of my room, in a bizarre way I felt free. As I write these words nearly four decades later, I recall my feelings of confusion and isolation with near-perfect clarity. As time went on, my drug dependence increased as its effectiveness at making me feel safe diminished. I became depressed and anxious, which I tried to keep to myself. I feared being found out, yet I felt more alone than ever. I had become too good at masking my pain.

Accepting and Embracing the Life We Have Lived

Today, when I want to get a good picture of just how afraid of intimacy I was, yet how much I yearned for it, I recall an incident that occurred when I was fifteen. I had just received my largest body cast yet. The thick, cold plaster went from my pelvis to over my head. I was in bed, in traction, with weights hanging from my waist, neck, and jaw. I had been receiving an injection of a narcotic every four hours for several weeks. My hospital bed command post had become a fortress, and my feelings lay safely buried deep beneath layers of plaster and obscured by a fog of drugs. Because of the traction weights I could barely open my mouth to speak.

One day, as I lay immobilized in bed, I watched the news on TV. On the screen was a baby girl who lived in a bubble. She had an immunodeficiency and could be touched (even by her parents) only through thick plastic gloves. The tragedy of her situation finally pierced the walls of my self-made fortress, and I sobbed as I watched her story unfold. I felt then, and I feel today, that I know too well the pain in the heart of that child.

My hospitalizations decreased as I approached the age of twenty, yet I continued to use drugs, which by this time included cocaine and alcohol. I did have periods of not using drugs, but I would always return to them when I got too close to someone. The drugs gave me a false sense of closeness to people while at the same time keeping them at a safe distance. I was trapped in a precarious balancing act that had been created years earlier by a young boy looking for a little attention.

It has been decades since I've used drugs. Looking back on it, I would not trade my life history for anyone else's. Today I am able to tell you I now know what true freedom is, and that I can and do experience deep emotions without reverting back to the Addictive Personality. The life that I have lived has taught me about addiction of all kinds, and I continue to find that it is possible to love and be loved in the moment, as I am. My experiences have shown me that there are two fundamental ways of being in the world: one is based on fear, the other on love. Today, I embrace and accept the life that I have lived, am grateful for its lessons, and now choose the way of love.

**The biggest waste of your time is wishing things had been different.
Instead, accept, embrace, learn, and create something wonderful
from this point on.**

Finding Freedom and Opportunity
through Responsibility

As children, we rarely consciously choose our roles. In our families of origin some of us become quiet and withdrawn, so much so that people barely knew we were there. Others of us become the high-achieving stars. Some of us become the "sensitive" children, taking on our families' pain. Others become the family clown, always joking around to draw attention away from our real feelings or the real situation. It is important for us to see how we may still be playing out the roles we adopted as children, even though they may prevent us from experiencing happiness and seeing opportunity. The good news is that as adults we can examine and change unwanted and outdated roles.

I choose the roles by which I live.
I choose the feelings that I experience.

In healing the Addictive Personality we can practice being flexible in our thinking, identify the roles we take, and develop the ability to change our lives by shifting our perception of ourselves and the world. It is important as adults that we make the decision to stop being on autopilot and instead make new and conscious choices. This is how I would define becoming responsible for our own lives. It is also how we discover opportunity.

There was a time that I would slump my shoulders at the word *responsibility*. I thought of responsibility as being connected with something I had to do but didn't really want to do. I also usually associated the word *should* with responsibility. I have come to see that there is another way to look at responsibility. It is my belief now that with true responsibility comes freedom. It was only when I decided to take responsibility for my own life and finally stopped compulsively blaming other people that I was able to start making decisions about my own life that really made a difference. Think of responsibility as a path to healing the Addictive Personality.

To heal old patterns, respond to each situation
from making new choices.
Responsibility is really the "ability-to-respond."
With this we have freedom.

The Big Myth: "I'm Not Okay the Way I Am"

Drugs were not my only escape route. I also found that I could create really lofty goals for myself and then hide in my pursuit of them. My "achievements" were really no different than the drugs I took: both kept my uncomfortable feelings at a comfortable distance. And much of the time I was under double sedation: I chased a goal *and* medicated myself to relieve the stress involved in my pursuit of the goal. Corporate America is full of this behavior.

Like many adolescents, I left high school confused about who I was. Within a few weeks of my arrival at the University of Oregon I was in a deep depression. I found that I could stave off the depression by getting lost in my work, so I began to immerse myself in my studies. Being overly studious appeared more acceptable than taking drugs, but for me they served the same purpose. I transferred later that year to Sonoma State University, which was near to my home in California. I believed the assertions of the Addictive Personality, that being there would help me to be happy. I found out that geographical moves are rarely the cure for depression. We take our thoughts and beliefs with us wherever we go.

I had no idea who I was or the purpose of what I was doing, but I was doing it exceedingly well and fast. I continued to excel at school and graduated from the four-year Bachelors-degree program before two years had passed with high honors. So on I went to graduate from college at nineteen years of age.

The Addictive Personality puts all its emphasis on what you do and none on who you are. In my family, working long and hard meant that you were doing something right; my father routinely put in twelve-hour days. And I set out to do the same. I was under the illusion that if "what" I was doing was seen as okay, the "who" I was becoming wouldn't matter very much. This error in thinking is fundamental to the Addictive Personality. It is the foundation in becoming a workaholic, and it is responsible for many ethical violations in business and politics.

The Misuse of Goals

Most people agree that having goals is a positive thing. However, with hard honesty I saw that my goals were anything but a positive force in my life. I built myself a rotating reward machine, based on my parents' prototype. As long as I focused on the reward that was tantalizingly just out of reach, I didn't have to deal with my shame, guilt, and low self-worth. As I pursued my goal, my machine would bring it closer and closer, and just as I was about to grab, my machine would drop it and produce a new one, again, just out of reach. My machine had an audio component as well. I could hear applause when I successfully reeled in a reward, which gave me at least temporary satisfaction. As time went on, the machine ran faster and faster, until one day I could no longer keep up the pace. I fell to the ground and lay there alone, my machine broken beyond repair from the fall. There was no one to applaud, just me, and I wept. I wept because I knew at that moment I would never again be able to hide in my pursuit of my unattainable goals. I lay alone with my fears. It was from my despair that I remembered who I was, a human being, and I started on the path of recognizing my essential value, recognition that had been lost in the pursuit of my endless goals.

Stopping the Cycle of Attack and Defense

In a world based on separation and scarcity, attack and defense seem like appropriate tools for survival. Attack and defense are upheld by the false belief that we are something other than love. If we practiced Recognized Essential Value, we would never need to attack. But if our self-esteem is measured by how much we have or what we are doing, then we naturally become fearful that what we have could be taken away or what we're doing might be stopped. When we draw arbitrary lines and divide the world into "good" people and "bad"' people, we must find ways to prove that our divisions are valid. We play judge and jury, passing verdicts and imposing sentences hundreds of times a day. When we see threats we launch our defense system. This scenario is based on the insane belief system that we are not okay the way we are. The truth needs to be repeated in many forms and often:

Our essential value needs no defense.

The Addictive Personality tells us that defense is our key to safety. Now let us look with hard honesty at what defense actually is.

The world has drawn boundaries to signify where one country begins and another ends. Each nation decides for itself whether another country was "friend" or "foe." Of course, who is currently an enemy may one day be an ally and vice versa. In our own country we have the tendency to see ourselves as always good and always right. Once our borders are in place we become concerned that another nation could threaten our territory. With fear as our leader, "self defense" seems totally reasonable. But there is one truth that our Addictive Personality keeps from us:

Our defenses bring what they were meant to guard against.

This is evident even on a global level: we tell ourselves that we must increase our defense systems to avoid future attack. But instead of making us feel safer, we tend to feel more vulnerable with each new weapon that is built. The likelihood of war actually increases because of the risk of accidental deployment and increased fear among our neighbors, often leading to accelerated weapons production of their own.

The same process occurs on an individual level. As we allow the Addictive Personality to compulsively build our individual defenses, we increase the likelihood of conflict. It is an unfortunate and vicious cycle: we feel afraid, so we build defenses; as we build defenses, we become more afraid.

The pattern builds momentum into an ongoing cycle of attack and defense where security, safety, and intimacy are virtually impossible.

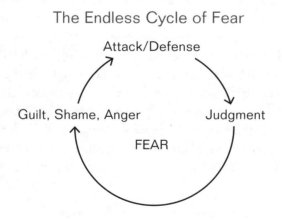

The Endless Cycle of Fear

Attack/Defense

Guilt, Shame, Anger   Judgment

FEAR

A Truth–Centered Approach to Life

As we heal the Addictive Personality we see that we can choose a different way of being in the world, and a different way of responding to challenging situations. Whereas the Addictive Personality makes relationships very complicated by endlessly analyzing and judging, the Truth-Based Personality cuts through all the diversions and distractions and sees the essence of human communication. The truth is that there are only two forms of communication. As a psychologist, when this idea first came to me it flew in the face of my education; millions of pages have been written on the various aspects and problems in communication, and I feel as though I've read them all! I have come to fully believe that seeing only two forms of communication is not an oversimplification. Whereas the Addictive Personality utilizes projection of the past into the present and future as a means of understanding and responding to communication, the Truth-Based Personality utilizes "extension," which is extending Recognized Essential Value from the moment.

Let's face it, when people are feeling bad about themselves, threatened, or afraid, it would be unusual for them to say in a calm voice, "I would like for you to recognize my essential value." On the contrary, they usually display some form of defensive or offensive behavior. Think how differently you might relate to other people if you saw them, and yourself, through the gentle and forgiving eyes that come from Recognized Essential Value. Such a truth-centered view of the world is based on acceptance and extension, as opposed to attack and defense, and on forgiveness, as opposed to judgment.

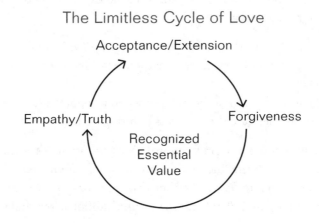

The Limitless Cycle of Love

Acceptance/Extension

Empathy/Truth

Forgiveness

Recognized
Essential
Value

The Truth about Anger, Guilt, Attack, and Defense

I become angry when another person doesn't live up to my expectations. The Addictive Personality fills your mind with "shoulds" and "oughts," and the result is anger and resentment. It enters into relationships with the mottoes: "Fulfill my expectations and I will accept you," or: "I will be happy if you. . ." When our peace of mind depends on another's behavior, sooner or later we will be disappointed. If we listen to the Addictive Personality, our usual response to this disappointment is anger and blame. One may be somewhat passive with their anger and withdraw, saying, "I don't want to get hurt again," or even make an apology of some kind. Some may be more aggressive, blaming and attacking the other person, saying, "I'm not happy and it's your fault." Either way, we are operating on the irrational addictive principles that happiness comes from another person, and they should and ought to behave the way we want them to at all times. The Truth-Based Personality is not so complicated and operates from a much simpler formula for happiness:

I am responsible for my happiness.
It is my responsibility to recognize opportunity.

- **When I become angry and attack another person, my hidden goal is to make the other person feel guilty.** In the Addictive Personality we have the absurd belief that:

  - Somebody else is responsible for how I feel.
  - Making another feel guilty for what he or she has done will make me feel better.

Utilize hard honesty and ask yourself right now: When has blaming ever given me lasting happiness? When did blaming ever show me new opportunity?

Mahatma Gandhi famously said that when you point a finger in blame at someone else, there are three fingers pointing back at yourself.

- **Attack and defense stem from not recognizing my essential value, which is love.** During the times in my life when I found myself verbally attacking or manipulating another person, it was never because I felt good about myself. What I craved was unconditional love and intimacy, exactly what my defenses kept me from experiencing. I have found it helpful, when I am caught up in a cycle of attack and defense, to ask myself, "What am I defending against? Could I practice Recognized Essential Value instead?" The Truth-Based Personality recognizes:

> Within me, within you, is essential value.
> There is nothing else I really need to know.

- **Projection is the means I use to justify attack.** Many times in our relationships, we see unwanted or denied aspects of ourselves manifesting in other people. I call this projection. The Addictive Personality uses projection to make us feel justified in attacking others. As we choose to become aware of who we are, we also must confront those repressed parts within us. I refer to this as owning our projections. In so doing we clean the lens through which we see others, and ultimately ourselves. The Truth-Based Personality recognizes that:

> Projection is the means the Addictive Personality
> uses to justify attack.
> But attack is never justified.
> Extension is the means by which
> the Truth-Based Personality uses to recognize myself.

- **Defenses always bring what they were meant to guard against.** Although the Addictive Personality tells us that our defenses make us safe, in reality our defenses are like a magnet, attracting exactly what they were designed to keep away. If I tell you, "Don't think of pink elephants," what does your mind do? It can't help but to think of pink elephants. This is similar to how our defenses work.

  - Every time we attack another person, we injure ourselves.
  - Whenever we are defensive, we are turning our backs on the opportunity to recognize the essential value (love) within ourselves and others.
  - It is our defensiveness that keeps us feeling separate and alone.
  - As long as we are in the cycle of attacking and defending, we are stuck in an addictive cycle.

Attack is a form of defense, and defenses bring what they were meant to guard against. When we attack another person, we are see our projections from the past, rather than recognize the essential value in the moment, and, thus, we hurt ourselves.

Punching your reflection in the mirror hurts your hand.

- **Anger, guilt, attack, and defense never bring me what I really want and always bring conflict.** If what you want is to be happy and to have opportunity in your life, you must realize that anger, guilt, attack, and defense only result in conflict. Always question the logic of the Addictive Personality, which states that we are in constant need of defense. The truth is that our safety lies in our defenselessness.

Healing the Addictive Personality is not always easy and requires a major shift in our thinking. The daily lessons that you will soon be doing do not give you specific rules for behavior, nor do they adhere to any specific dogma. Rules and dogma are not that hard to follow, but rarely result in deep change. In this book I am asking you for much more. *A Course in Miracles* states: "If you want peace, you must give up the idea of conflict entirely and for all time." In other words, if you want the uninterrupted peace of the Truth-Based Personality, you must give up the Addictive Personality for all time. This is not, obviously, easy to do. In another passage from the *Course* it states, "If you forget, try again. If there are long interruptions, try again. Whenever you remember, try again." Two simple statements can put me back on the path to living from the Truth-Based Personality.

Defensiveness brings fear.
Defenselessness brings love.

- **Attack and defense preserve guilt and escalate fear.** Guilt and fear keep the wheels of the Addictive Personality turning. The Addictive Personality tells us that fear is real and that we are in constant danger. We play the game of hot potato, where we quickly toss our guilt to the next person, thinking that we are getting rid of it.

If I want to be happy, I must see that
tossing my guilt to another person does not get rid of it.

- **Attack and defense are a call for us to recognize the essential value in ourselves and others.** Throughout my career I have worked with the wealthy and the poor, CEOs and the homeless, prisoners and politicians, gang members and gurus. I have concluded that there is one commonality among them: There is no one who does not want to experience love. The problem is that because of the Addictive Personality we can become confused and think we are protecting ourselves, when we are actually keeping love away and fear alive. As hard as it is to see, when someone behaves defensively, it is really a cry for help. If you can respond by practicing Recognized Essential Value, the cycle will eventually cease.

Where there is fear, love is the answer.

- **Forgiveness is the key to happiness.** My friend, Beverly Hutchinson-McNeff, said after thirty years of focused spiritual practice, "People can look at me and think one of two things: 'She is pretty enlightened' or, 'She is a very slow learner.'" I can relate, and, like her, tend to feel the latter is true. Healing and growth come from truths that we either adopt or avoid.

Accept responsibility for your experiences and actions,
and live a life allowing forgiveness to lead the way.

This is vastly more challenging than following rules, dogma, or just repeating positive affirmations. Happiness and recognizing new opportunity begin with a change in how we perceive the world and ourselves. Forgiveness is the gentle letting go of the past. It allows us to view the world and ourselves through the clarity of the present moment. We are constantly choosing between forgiveness and the cycle of attack and defense.

Forgiveness is my single function
when peace of mind is my single goal.

Trust Versus trust

Even after reading the preceding points, there will still be people or situations that may be dishonest, cruel, violent, and abusive that should be stopped and may be hard to forgive. To address this dilemma, it is important to discuss the facets of trust.

There are actually two types of trust: Trust with a capital "T" and trust with a lowercase "t." Trust is based on Recognized Essential Value. It comes with knowing that we can see the value, the love, in a person without having to also approve or condone their behavior. This helps us let go of our need to control them. Think of the other trust as based on consistency of behavior. People need to show us they can be trusted to do what they say in order for us to trust them. What's more, we can recognize the essential value in another person and still hold them accountable for their actions. We don't have to defend our hearts from love because we fear someone's behavior. When we take our interactions with others to this higher level, we are Trusting with a capital T. Forgiveness is a natural extension of this kind of Trust because we are looking beyond behavior and into the heart of the person. Remember:

- I can always recognize the essential value in other people, regardless of their behavior. This is Trust, and forgiveness is much easier from here.

- Other people's behavior is about them, not about me. Let me take responsibility for my feelings and actions and allow others to do the same.

- I cannot control or predict other people's actions. I can choose between building a fence around my heart and seeing the value (love) of others and myself.

Learning to Recognize Our Essential Value

Learning to Recognize Essential Value is to learn to love yourself; this is the basis for release from the cycle of suffering caused by the Addictive Personality. You cannot have opposing goals and expect to be happy (or sane). Compulsively searching outside yourself while trying to recognize essential value are mutually exclusive. In other words, you cannot maintain certain aspects of your addictive lifestyle and fully love yourself. If you don't fully love yourself, you cannot realize your happiness or new opportunity. It is my belief that much addictive behavior continues because we don't take this to heart, and instead of fully letting go of the Addictive Personality we play a version of "Let's Make a Deal." We play the game because we are still focused on controlling, acquiring, judging, defending, and attacking. We don't see the cycle of suffering, and thus continue in it as though it will bring us happiness and safety.

The truth is that our addictions become the walls behind which we hide. Eventually, they become so high that instead of simply hiding behind them we become prisoners of our own making. The bars of our cells are forged with the irrational beliefs of the Addictive Personality. We sit on cold gray cement in our dark and isolated cells, believing there is no escape.

In order to heal the Addictive Personality and recognize our essential value, we must first identify the irrational beliefs that keep us stuck where we are.

What the Addictive Personality Wants You to Believe

- **My self-esteem is dependent upon everyone else's approval at all times.** Because unanimous approval is highly unlikely, this belief results in another one of the Addictive Personality's vicious cycles:

  - I try to please other people so I will feel good about myself.

  - I eventually fail because I can't always please everybody. Failure brings on feelings of guilt, which lead to feelings of low self-worth.

  - To compensate for feelings of low self-worth, I become even more of a people pleaser.

In the Truth-Based Personality I realize that

  - My self-esteem comes from recognizing my essential value and is not dependent upon pleasing others.

  - Approval seeking takes me away from who I am.

  - Recognizing Essential Value takes me to who I am.

- **If I am to consider myself worthwhile, I must excel, achieve, win, and display glowing competence at all times, in all places, and at all costs.** Is it any surprise that such a belief leads to addiction? This belief is based on the fear that if you let down your guard for even a second you might slip up and be found to be incompetent. The fear of being discovered as an imposter is all too prevalent in our society. Some years ago, I read a fascinating study that described some of my most deeply hidden fears. The study revealed that a large number of individuals in high-profile professional positions felt deep down that they were not qualified to do their jobs, were afraid that one day they might be unmasked as frauds, and took great pains to hide their perceived inadequacies. This was me for so much of my life. But the Truth-Based Personality reflects the actual truth about who we are:

> My self-worth is not based solely upon what I do or achieve.
> I am enough right now.

- **All things that go wrong in my life are caused by other people. These people need to be blamed and punished.** To avoid our own underlying feelings of inadequacy we may blame other people. When we feel out of control we irrationally think that blame and punishment will somehow restore order, so we blame someone else before they have the chance to blame us. Fear is at the core of this belief, which makes us blind to the source of the problem: the irrational beliefs of the Addictive Personality. By contrast, the Truth-Based Personality recognizes that:

> Healing must begin in my own mind.
> Blaming and relentless punishment perpetuate the problem.

- **If external situations in my life are not exactly how I want them to be, I must feel stressed-out, worry endlessly, and expect a disaster to occur any moment.** A surefire way to keep us from looking in the mirror and acknowledging our belief systems is to become totally preoccupied with the chaos and drama around us, leaving no time for anything else. Although we now know that the situation does *not* determine the experience, you, like me, may have gotten used to feeling happy when things go your way, and unhappy when they don't. I behaved like a robot with a programmed response for every situation, rather than a person with free will and a mind of my own. I was so caught up in trying to control my external world and relationships that I forgot about my inner life. The compulsive need to control external circumstances guarantees a life devoid of lasting peace and opportunity.

I took pottery classes for several years, which I found very enjoyable. Centering the clay on the wheel required just the right amount of pressure. Once the clay was centered, and the pot began to form, releasing the pressure even for a moment allowed centrifugal force to throw it off balance and turn it back into a misshapen lump of clay. Trying to control our external world is not dissimilar. The thing about trying to control every situation is that the job is never quite done, and it feels as if it's always a second away from falling apart. If we relax even for a moment everything could collapse. Besides, we will always be able to find something else that needs to be controlled. However, as we become more aware of the truth of who we are, the need to control the external world diminishes.

It may sound like I am advocating, "Don't give a darn about anything except yourself." This is not what I am saying. It is the Addictive Personality that promotes the myth that compulsive control is effective. I am, in fact, an advocate for offering service to the world. But, this is not from a place of trying to control the world, but rather from a place of compassion and tenderness toward the world.

Because the focus of this book is on our thinking, it is worth saying again that I am not suggesting that we should not care about what is happening in the world. I am saying that where we must begin is where we must also end.

> If I want to change my life, I must first change my mind.
> What I experience is based upon my thoughts and beliefs.
> What I can bring to the world is compassion rather than control.

- **If something negative happened in the past, I should be very concerned about it repeating itself in the future.** Despite the power of the human mind, many of us have problems with three simple facts about time: The past is past. The future is the future. The present is present. There is nothing etched in stone that states that the past will repeat itself, yet many people run their lives on this premise, which leads to a lack of trust and guardedness. When we are so concerned about the past we tend to overlook the opportunity in the present. This is a known fact in science and is referred to as "experimenter bias." It has been demonstrated that if the experimenter is looking for something specific to happen, that is often what will be found, or at least observed over other data occurring simultaneously. For much of my life, when I saw my negative predictions come true my commitment to worrying about the next catastrophe increased proportionally in an endless vicious cycle.

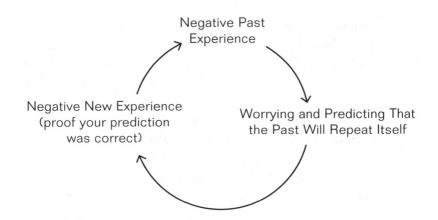

Negative Past Experience

Negative New Experience (proof your prediction was correct)

Worrying and Predicting That the Past Will Repeat Itself

Excessive worry does far more harm than good. This phenomenon has been demonstrated in extensive research in the field of health psychology. People who are excessively fearful of becoming sick can actually increase their risk for health problems. Today, few health professionals would deny that mental attitude plays a vital role in physical well-being and recovery from illness and injury. This area fascinates me and is the subject of my next book, in which I focus on finding the silver lining in our physical challenges, rather than on being a passive and fearful victim.

> Because of the power of thought
> we attract that upon which we dwell.
> This power can be used to bring
> either positive or negative experiences into our life.
> The choice is ours.

- **If I avoid painful issues and repress my emotions, I will be safe and happy.** Through our addictions we attempt to repress our feelings of anger, unworthiness, and shame. When we stop our addictive behavior by confronting our Addictive Personality, repressed pain, and even existential despair, may rise to the surface. It is by having the courage to allow this process to unfold (perhaps with the help of a friend, therapist, sponsor, coach, or mentor) and to work through the pain that we once again become open to our feelings and, finally, fully human. Procrastination and avoidance are indirect ways of saying, "I don't trust myself, my intuition, or the unfolding of my life."

Our pain makes us afraid to move in any direction; we become stuck. The more fearful we become, the more we procrastinate. As we procrastinate we adopt more addictive ways of being in order to further avoid our feelings and create more reasons to dislike ourselves.

The Addictive Personality states:
Avoidance + Repression + Projection = Safety and Opportunity

The Truth-Based Personality states:
Courage + Awareness + Extension = Safety and Opportunity

- **I am weak and I need to be dependent on somebody or something else.** If you feel weak, incomplete, or somehow insufficient, even being alone for a few hours may make you uncomfortable. You may find that food, alcohol, drugs, or addictive behaviors give you temporary relief, yet deep down the feeling of incompleteness persists.

When I was a kid, I enjoyed doing jigsaw puzzles with my family. Sometimes, when we couldn't find a piece, even after a prolonged search, we would joke that the puzzle must have been sent from the manufacturer with a piece missing. Each time this happened I became convinced that someone at the factory had a cruel sense of humor and had withheld one or two pieces. Eventually, of course, the missing piece would always turn up.

None of us came into this world with pieces missing. It may take patience and perseverance to remember and rediscover our innate wholeness, but it is there. Try living by this truth, and see how different your life becomes.

This is not to say that we don't grow and benefit from intimacy with other people. But being in a dependent position is not intimacy, it is dependence and is based on a belief that we lack something. We become needy because this is how we think we will attract and keep someone. It is also worth mentioning that the reverse is also the case: we have to feel needed to feel whole. Here the false assumption is that if we can fulfill the needs of someone else, we will attract and keep them, possibly forever.

The solution is to become aware of our wholeness and to be open to giving and receiving true nurturing and support. Only then can we begin to truly share ourselves with others, and only then can we attract healthy people into our lives.

> Stop looking to another person
> to make up for a perceived lack in yourself.
> Stop needing to be needed
> to make up for a perceived lack in yourself.
> Know that you are whole.
> Give and receive, and you will attract amazing people
> and new opportunity into your life.

- **I should be very involved in, and upset about, other people's problems.** When I was in practice full time as a psychologist, people often asked "Don't you get depressed listening to peoples' problems all day?" I would suggest to them that it is possible to be of service to others without taking on their issues or their pain. When I had a "good day" it was not because my clients had fewer problems, it was because on that particular day I was pretty good at practicing Recognized Essential Value. This is an important differentiation. We always have the choice to either become involved in the drama of other people or to practice seeing their true value. The latter is always helpful, whereas the former rarely is.

Each of us can be compassionate without taking on suffering. If you believe what the Addictive Personality promotes, you may think that being helpful means being overly identified with another person's pain. Though it is important to acknowledge their pain, it is equally important to see that person's essential value, which is their strength.

> When you see the underlying strength and wholeness
> in another person,
> you both will feel whole, strong, and enlivened.
> When you identify only with their pain,
> you both will feel only pain and exhaustion.

When I first entered graduate school, I was not at all clear about this process. In fact, my Addictive Personality sold me on the belief that I was less than whole and that the way to feel good about myself, even powerful, was to find people and situations that needed to be fixed. What better way than becoming a psychologist! The truth, at least in part, was that I tried to solve other people's problems as a way of giving myself some self-esteem. And this was just another form of addiction: I thought that doing something positive for someone else would make *me* feel whole. When I finally let go of the idea that I had to be a super problem-solver, I initially experienced some shame that the addiction had covered up. But as I continued to move into the Truth-Based Personality's role of Recognizing Essential Value, I finally was able to be of real service.

Fixing you will not fix me.
Recognizing your true strength solidifies yours and mine.

- **There is one right way to view the world.** To compensate for some of the craziness and inconsistencies that we are surrounded by, you may protect yourself by seeing the world as divided into good and bad, right and wrong. The subtext of this belief is "My safety lies in believing that everything is black and white, that there are no gray areas in life." Recognizing that this rigid view of the world lacks truth may bring your underlying anxiety to the surface. This is because when you give up rigidity you must embrace life's ambiguities.

Conflicts, ranging from family strife to work-related arguments or from partisan politics to war, are born from rigid closed-mindedness. We can become addicted to a certain way of viewing the world, even though that view keeps us from experiencing closeness with others or a peaceful and secure existence. Whenever you are in conflict, remember:

There is another way to look at this.
The world is not always clearly black and white.
If I am attached to being right,
I am shutting the door on new opportunities
and important life lessons.

- **I am limited in what I can do, what I can have, and the happiness that I can experience.** There is an entire vocabulary devoted to the belief that people are limited. Each and every day these words virtually stop our minds from being able to create and/or recognize opportunity. I refer to these words as "opportunity blockers." An opportunity blocker is the mortar that holds the bricks of the fear-based Addictive

Personality together. If we remove the mortar (opportunity blockers), the bricks (fear-based beliefs) are more easily removed, and healing takes place. Some examples of opportunity blockers follow in a paragraph that illustrates how the Addictive Personality puts them to use.

"I doubt if I could ever succeed at having the life I want. What if I try and fail? I know that I should do certain things, but my life is just too difficult. And I shouldn't try anything that would cause me to make a mistake. Besides, nobody else seems to be able to succeed at much; it is impossible to overcome certain obstacles. And I've tried it all before; I can't do it. If only things were different now, or had been different in the past. I ought to be able to do better, but I have this limitation that prevents me. Nothing I do will ever be enough. Besides, I don't have enough time or money to do so."

Words to watch for in your thinking and conversation:

I doubt
I should
but
difficult
I shouldn't
impossible
I've tried
I can't
if only
I ought
limitation
nothing
not enough time or money
never enough

We've all used these words without even realizing it. With conscious effort we can eliminate them from our thinking and our vocabulary. In doing so we will make giant strides toward healing the Addictive Personality.

In his book, *Illusions,* Richard Bach wrote one sentence that perfectly summarizes opportunity blockers:

"Argue for your limitations and sure enough, they're yours."

The following lists repeat the irrational beliefs of the Addictive Personality and the peaceful alternatives of the Truth-Based Personality. You may find it helpful to refer to them in times of conflict to see your choices, and/or read the messages from the Truth-Based Personality on a daily basis to set your thinking in the desired direction.

Irrational Beliefs of the Addictive Personality

1. My self-esteem is dependent on the approval of others.

2. If I am to consider myself worthwhile, I must excel, achieve, win, and display glowing competence at all times, in all places, and at all costs.

3. Everything that goes wrong in my life is caused by other people. These people must be blamed and punished.

4. If external situations in my life are not exactly how I want them to be, I must feel stressed-out, constantly worried, and expect a disaster to occur any moment.

5. If something negative happened in the past, I should be very concerned about it repeating in the future.

6. If I avoid painful issues and repress down my emotions, I will be safe and happy.

7. I am weak and need to be dependent on somebody or something else.

8. I should be very involved in, and very upset about, other people's problems.

9. There is one right way to view the world.

10. I am limited in what I can do, what I can have, and the happiness I can experience.

Alternate Messages from the Truth-Based Personality

1. My self-esteem comes from recognizing my essential value.
   It is not dependent upon pleasing others.

2. My self-worth is not based solely upon what I do or achieve.
   I am enough right now.

3. Healing must begin in my own mind.
   Blaming and punishment perpetuate the problem.

4. If I want to change my life, I must first change my mind.
   What I experience is based upon my thoughts and beliefs.

5. Because of the power of thought I attract that upon which I dwell.
   This power can be used to bring either positive or negative experiences into my life.

6. Courage + Awareness + Extension = Safety and Happiness.

7. I am whole, I am able to give and receive, and I attract amazing people into my life.

8. When I see strength and wholeness in a person, I feel whole, strong, and enlivened.
   When I identify only with the pain, I feel pain and exhaustion.

9. The world is not always clearly black and white.
   If I am attached to always being right, I shut the door to new opportunities.

10. I am limitless.

Being Compulsively-Other-Focused

There are many labels and terms unique to the fields of psychology and addiction. In my book *Healing the Addictive Mind*, I described codependency as a constellation of emotions, beliefs, and behaviors based on the individual's feelings of shame, low self-worth, and fear of intimacy. Since then I have come to see that it is more useful to be descriptive rather than diagnostic when approaching certain aspects of the Addictive Personality. I feel it is more empowering for people to see the results of their thinking and then do something different. Thus, I don't use the word codependency much anymore. Today, I prefer the more descriptive phrase "compulsively-other-focused" (COF), which describes the pervasive way the Addictive Personality maintains its fundamental belief in control.

In the end, control becomes an elusive project. Ironically, once we are addicted to someone or something, we spend most of our energy trying to control its availability and behavior. The Addictive Personality in turn uses denial to reassure ourselves that we're in control of the addiction. Thus the addiction and our need to appear in control become partners, making peace of mind impossible.

When you try to control another person's behavior,
lasting peace of mind for yourself is impossible.

When you are compulsively-other-focused you are often exhausted, as if you are on the last mile of a marathon. Because it takes so much effort to maintain the façade, however, you may not appear to be tired. But later, as you heal you will look back and laugh at how much energy it took to look as though everything were fine.

Some years ago, Sally Anne came to see me after she attended a workshop where I spoke about the Addictive Personality and being compulsively-other-focused. She had identified with much of the material presented and wanted to take a more in-depth look at her life. Sally Anne was forty-two, had grown up in a workaholic home, and was married to a recovering alcoholic. She was what most of us would call a "responsible" person; she worked a demanding job and was raising two children. She spent a great deal of time taking care of other people and almost no time taking care of herself. She was also dedicated to worrying about and trying to limit her husband's drinking. As our work progressed, Sally Anne found that her self-esteem was tied to trying to solve other people's problems, seeking approval from others, and relieving other people's pain. She routinely put other people's needs and feelings first, at the expense of her own. Despite her initial reluctance to see it, Sally Anne found herself lonely and unhappy in a life where guilt and shame were her primary feelings, and control and manipulation were the primary behaviors.

It was at a very early age that Sally Anne assumed responsibility for other people's feelings. As a young child, when one of her parents got angry, Sally Anne would feel responsible. When something embarrassing happened in public that was related to her parent's drinking, she felt the humiliation that her parents seemed oblivious to. As an adult, when her husband did something that compromised her values, she felt the shame that he apparently did not. Regardless of how strong her feelings were, she rarely expressed them, because she was too worried about the other person's reaction. As Sally Anne became more and more caught up in this cycle of being compulsively-other-focused, she became less and less aware of her true feelings. By the time she attended that first workshop she was not sure what she felt anymore and had difficulty identifying or expressing any opinions of her own.

Much of Sally Anne's difficulty came from the belief that she didn't have a right to her feelings or a life she could call her own. She always put others first, always at the expense of her own growth, which is not real giving at all. When it came to her family, it was as though she had radar and knew how everyone would react and when a conflict might be brewing. The problem was that she could rarely identify her own feelings or needs. As our work together progressed, Sally Anne's awareness increased. Long-buried fears of rejection, loneliness, and shame came into focus for the first time in many years.

After working with Sally Anne and many others, I have come to realize that being compulsively-other-focused is clearly an addiction in its own right. The list that follows states the core beliefs that I consider to be the bedrock of being compulsively-other-focused followed by the feeling or characteristic that results from each belief.

Ten Core Beliefs of Being Compulsively-Other-Focused

1. **Belief:** I am responsible for other people's feelings and behaviors. What other people do is a reflection of who I am.

   Result: I feel guilty much of the time. I feel good about myself only when everyone else is okay.

2. **Belief:** Other people's lives and feelings are more important than my own.

   Result: I have a hard time taking care of myself and identifying my feelings. I often question what I feel, I hardly ever say no, and I feel guilty when I do.

3. **Belief:** I have to be needed by others in order to feel loved and worthwhile.

   Result: I choose relationships in which I take care of others but rarely receive nurturing myself. I put other people's needs and desires first. I feel guilty if I take any time just for me. I confuse being needed with being loved. I can be there for everybody except myself. Sometimes I feel extremely resentful and angry.

4. **Belief:** Other people's opinions and values are more important than my own.

   Result: I am not aware of having my own opinions, and those that I do have I am afraid to express. I find it difficult to make decisions. I am like a sponge, absorbing what others feel, think, and value. I sometimes feel completely lost. I don't know who I am or what I want.

5. **Belief:** I don't have the right to my own feelings.

   Result: I fear other people's reactions to my feelings and behavior, especially their anger. I am a compulsive worrier about what other people think of me. I try to do the "right" thing, but I never feel authentic, trusting, present, or appreciated for who I am. I feel small and powerless. I often feel afraid and/or resentful. I deny my values and repress feelings in order to feel accepted by others. I have never felt heard or accepted.

6. **Belief:** My relationships with others reflect who I am. Likewise, their behavior toward me reflects who I am.

   Result: I am afraid of being rejected, and because of this it is hard for me to feel close to other people. If my relationships are good, I feel okay for a while; when trouble arises, my life falls apart. I have a confused view of loyalty, and thus I am loyal to a fault, which means I remain loyal even when it is harmful to me or someone else.

7. **Belief:** I should be ashamed.

   Result: I minimize my feelings and try to please others in order to avoid my feelings of low self-worth. I can't let others really get to know me, because they wouldn't like me if they knew me well. I don't feel worthy of love because, sooner or later, I always fall short of their expectations.

8. **Belief:** I need to dictate, manage, and control other people's behavior in order to feel safe and happy.

   Result: My peace of mind is determined by how others behave. I have difficulty recognizing or acknowledging good qualities in myself. I am always the peacekeeper, smoothing over any conflict, no matter the cost to me.

9. **Belief:** I am inadequate.

   Result: I must be able to justify my feelings. No matter what I do, I don't feel good enough. I never say no. I am always taking on tasks and projects in order to feel some sense of self-esteem. I am prone to being a workaholic. I'm afraid that if I let my guard down, someone will find out how incompetent I am.

10. **Belief:** I must be perfect at all times.

    Result: I continually watch and criticize my thoughts, and actions. I judge everything that I do, say, or even think with harshness. I am rarely, if ever, satisfied with my performance. Therefore I am full of self-condemnation and empty of self-love.

Whether or not you begin to open your life to the power of the Truth-Based Personality is up to you. Now that you have read and considered the material presented, I hope you will further consider making a serious practice of the Daily Lessons that follow in Chapter 8. To prepare for this, the following suggestions are ways in which you can, right now, begin to open the door to healing:

1. Choose to have the willingness, the openness, and the desire to view your life with hard honesty. Choose to feel your feelings.

2. Practice, many times a day, letting go of controlling other people, places, and things.

3. Affirm who you are with full consciousness (practice Recognized Essential Value).

Healing through Forgiveness

You will notice that periodically throughout this book I have discussed the importance of forgiveness. Because the Addictive Personality is quick to devalue the power of forgiveness, I have found that frequent reminders allow for a deeper understanding and experience.

Imagine what your house would look like (and smell like) if you never took out the garbage. Yet, you may go through life accumulating worries, negative beliefs about yourself, judgments, and miscellaneous other "trash talk." And when you are ready to go to sleep at night, you take your trashcan and empty the contents into your bed, and then you climb in between the garbage-strewn sheets. Upon waking you diligently stuff all the trash back in the can and set out on yet another day of trash collecting.

You have to remember to empty the can. It's time to take care of your true home, your heart, and your mind. It's time to identify and let go of your "garbage" thoughts. When you adopt a daily practice of letting go, you will naturally begin to feel more free, more present, and more effective in your life. I suggest returning to page 90 for daily Forgiveness Practice Sessions.

Letting Go . . .

By letting go we allow our lives to naturally unfold and bring us lessons, instead of trying to bring about a certain outcome.

By letting go we do not stop caring about other people, rather we see their true essence, unencumbered by our judgments, and we begin to care and respond to others with true compassion.

By letting go we realize that we can't control other people's behavior, but we can change how we perceive others and ourselves.

By letting go we see the essential value in people, instead of being fear-focused; thus we completely change our view of ourselves and everyone else.

By letting go we stop blaming others and we release our guilt. We can freely express our feelings and allow others to express theirs.

By letting go of control we practice extension of love rather than projection of guilt. In doing so we reduce our attachment to the outcome of situations that are beyond our control.

By letting go of judgment we allow ourselves and others to be fallible human beings. We realize that a judgmental mind is not a peaceful mind.

By letting go we see that holding onto a painful past is the last thing we want to do.

By letting go we end denial and allow all good things to express themselves.

By letting go we forgive ourselves and others, and we see opportunity where we once saw only pain and hopelessness.

Affirming Who You Are

Without conscious intention, we spend too much time unconsciously reinforcing the Addictive Personality. We engage in endless negative self-talk and rarely hold anything positive and true in our minds for more than a few moments. Then we wonder why we don't have the abundant life we want. When we look in the mirror, it may be easier to be self-critical than it is to see our essential value. Then we wonder why nobody seems to love us the way we want to be loved.

It is up to each of us to begin to cultivate who we really want to be. The list that follows offers affirmations that can help reverse negative self-talk. I suggest that you choose one affirmation each day and repeat it to yourself every waking hour for one minute. (You may need a reminder, such as the alarm setting on your wristwatch.) Note that the time devoted is a mere one-sixtieth of your waking day. Yet all that's needed is this small commitment.

Your essential value (love) has the same properties as light: when you enter a dark room and turn on a lamp, the darkness disappears; light fills the room. It is the same experience when you recognize who you really are: love fills your consciousness.

The affirmations that follow are specifically designed for those who see compulsively-other-focused traits in themselves. They are also universal concepts that can benefit anyone.

Truths about Myself

1. I am surrounded by love and opportunity. I am safe. There is nothing to fear.

2. I am worthwhile and able to succeed in life. I need do nothing today to prove myself worthy.

3. My feelings and my existence need no justification. Today I can feel and express my feelings constructively.

4. I am gentle with myself because I value who I am. Self-criticism only injures me.

5. I am not alone in my thinking, and aligning my thoughts with other positive people makes a difference.

6. The past is over. Letting go through forgiveness is how I create new opportunities in my life.

7. I choose my feelings. My happiness is not controlled by other people, places, or things.

8. I am valuable. Because of this I can take time for myself today without feeling guilty.

9. Peace of mind is always available to me. When I find myself in conflict I need but change my mind.

10. I deserve opportunity, am grateful for each one, and welcome more each day.

Healing Relationships: Growing Beyond the Addictive Personality in Our Interactions with Others

There are many excellent books on relationships, and I do not attempt to supersede them with this one very short chapter. However, I believe that certain aspects of healing relationships are an integral part of healing the Addictive Personality.

For years I assisted people with all types of relationship challenges, including career issues to marital problems. I often found that the individuals had lost sight of, or never knew in the first place, who they really were, who the other person was, what the purpose of the relationship was, or what was most important to them in life.

These individuals would often assert that they knew what they wanted, making statements such as "I just want to be listened to and shown a little respect," or, "I just want to hear a few words of appreciation for what I do instead of endless complaints and criticism." But most still clung to past drama and old patterns of anger and blame and had no real sense of themselves, each other, or what was really important to them. Some relationships deteriorate to an extreme of fear, guilt, defense, attack, and even violence.

When we operate in the Addictive Personality, we are like a rat in a maze. Each path promises a positive outcome, but each path chosen leads deeper into confusion and despair. If you want positive relationships you must be willing to go beyond the Addictive Personality to completely different territory. The goal is to see that each relationship has a purpose, and that purpose is to teach you more about your own true nature. With hard honesty you can rise above your fear, leave your old dysfunctional patterns behind, and relate to yourself and others in entirely new ways.

Though I could recount many stories of people with challenging relationships, including plenty from my own past, most of them have similar patterns that are rooted in the Addictive Personality. Though we may want to think that our problems are special and different, the truth is that they pretty much all stem from the same faulty thinking. Though this may not make us feel unique, it does make it easier to find real solutions. In order to experience more peace, personal growth, communication, and effectiveness in your relationships, consider the list that follows.

Six Core Truths of Truth-Based Relationships

1. **Know what you want to learn.**
   Know that the cycles of the Addictive Personality are learned patterns of relating and therefore can be unlearned. Know you want to learn about the Truth-Based Personality.

2. **Know what is possible and how to attract and manifest it.**
   Recognize that more loving and peaceful relationships are possible through practicing Recognized Essential Value.

3. **Know the purpose of every relationship.**
   Understand that the purpose of any relationship is to learn the lessons of kindness and compassionate action, not to reinforce and repeat a painful past.

4. **Know where to look for happiness and great relationships.**
   Make a conscious effort to be aware of your fears and hidden thoughts when you relate with others. When you see the Addictive

Personality playing its games, you will be better able to see, value, and cultivate the Truth-Based Personality.

5. **Know how to choose what you want now, rather than repeating your mistakes and old patterns.**
   Know and practice the three magical words that lay the groundwork for positive relationships to emerge. The phrase "Choose once again" can redirect your mind even if you are already caught in a negative cycle of the Addictive Personality. No matter how off center you may be, you have the power to redirect your mind, and therefore your relationships. For example, if you are in an angry cycle, you can learn to catch yourself, breathe, and mentally say, "Choose once again." This allows you to begin to shift your thinking from the Addictive Personality, thus creating closeness instead of separation.

6. **Know what is valuable and what is not.**
   Decide there is no value in guilt, and unlimited value in forgiveness. Pledge to practice forgiveness, and see this as the path to peace. Become a messenger of peace, instead of a messenger of guilt.

These six points of knowledge are straightforward, yet the Addictive Personality manifests itself in relationships through innumerable irrational thoughts. The list that follows compiles what I consider to be the five most common thoughts of the Addictive Personality that keep people from successful relationships. Following this list is another list with five parallel thoughts of the Truth-Based Personality. They can be applied to virtually any relationships, including those with friends, family, romantic partners, or co-workers. These lists are not meant to be comprehensive; feel free to add any thoughts of your own that come to mind.

Patterns of the Addictive Personality
That Create Conflict and Traps

- If I have to put effort into the relationship, something must be wrong.

- When there is disagreement, somebody has to be wrong. I should try my best to prove that something is not my fault. I should also keep score, making sure that I am right most of the time.

- If I pretend that everything is okay, it will be. If I ignore problems and feelings, things will improve.

- If I make other people feel guilty, it will make me feel better. Blaming is always a good defensive strategy.

- Whenever I give to someone in any regard, I should be able to expect something in return.

Patterns of the Truth–Based Personality
That Create Peace and Opportunity

- In our relationship it is my goal not to hide; I wish to be present and authentic with you.

- Looking beyond fault, there is no situation that is devoid of opportunity for growth.

- When I avoid or pretend, I turn my back on the opportunity to learn from you and deepen my relationship with you.

- My goal is to overcome guilt, not reinforce it; I do this through forgiveness.

- Every kind thought reinforces itself. Giving and receiving are the same thing.

Relationships are our classrooms; it is in our relationships where we have the greatest opportunity to learn how to live out the Truth-Based Personality. I have certainly found this to be true in my relationships.

All relationships are at their best when
we see the purpose is to learn and grow.

At its highest,
any relationship is motivated
by practicing recognized essential value,
and where we seek the truth in each event,
and act on that truth.

As we grow in understanding and acceptance
of ourself and whoever is in front of us,
we open our life to all opportunity.

It is through the intention to understand and forgive
that we find peace in every step.

You Are Not Alone: An Introduction to the Daily Lessons

Fifteen years ago, when I first wrote a series of twenty-one lessons, I never imagined that over 100,000 people would use them. Despite many generous testimonials praising their effectiveness, I have also gratefully received feedback on how to improve them. To this end I have tried to simplify each lesson and make each concept even more practical. Although all lesson titles are new and the content is applicable to healing the Addictive Personality, many of the central themes follow those presented in *A Course in Miracles* and *Healing the Addictive Mind*.

Imagine the collective power of one million people who are healing the Addictive Personality and are bringing into the world all that the Truth-Based Personality has to offer. With this book, I have the intention that the 100,000 people who have practiced these lessons will grow to one million. I share my intention for two reasons. First, so that even if you are practicing these lessons by yourself, you know that you are not alone. I hope you will allow the collective strength of others to uplift you throughout this challenging time. Second, so that you realize your practice is part of a much larger global healing that is taking place today through this and other compassion-based works. To help facilitate these goals, I have created a website that offers daily words of wisdom to support the lessons, as well as a place for you to connect with and mutually support other people practicing the same material. These two services are free of charge, and the website address is www.DrLeeJampolsky.com.

The exercises that follow offer you a systematic and practical means for living a life free of the Addictive Personality. Through this practice the Addictive Personality can be healed and the peace of mind of the Truth-Based Personality can be more consistently experienced. Do not worry about "believing in" all of the ideas presented here; simply be open to practicing them for a day and let your experience speak for itself.

The daily lessons and the discussions that accompany them are brief, practical, and direct. The emphasis is not on theory, but rather on experience. To receive the greatest benefit, proceed as follows: Each morning soon after rising, review the day's lesson and its accompanying discussion. Start with Lesson One and practice one lesson per day in sequence. Practice in a quiet place where you won't be disturbed. Relax, and spend about five minutes thoughtfully reading the lesson and accompanying discussion, then keep the lesson and discussion in the forefront of your thoughts. During your practice time concentrate on the lesson and the discussion, and if an unwanted thought interrupts your concentration, simply acknowledge its presence and then gently let it go.

Throughout the day, slowly and thoughtfully repeat the lesson to yourself. This is especially useful in times of conflict. It may not be appropriate to apply the lesson to *every* person and *all* situations that you encounter, but do not purposely make exceptions. Review the lesson periodically during the day for a few moments, preferably hourly. You may find it helpful either to carry the book with you or to copy the lesson onto a three-by-five card that you can slip into your pocket or purse.

In the evening, preferably just before retiring, take a few minutes to review the day's lesson and the discussion again. Think about your day and how the lesson applied to specific circumstances or relationships.

When you have completed all twenty-one lessons in this manner, it is helpful to begin again and repeat the series. A continuous practice is best maintained until you find yourself applying the lessons spontaneously and consistently.

Your daily practice consists of four parts: a morning practice session, application of the lesson to stressful situations that occur throughout the day, an hourly review, and an evening review.

DAILY LESSONS

ᴐ LESSON ONE

I give everything all the meaning it has for me.

Because this lesson completely contradicts the core beliefs of the Addictive Personality, it may be confusing at first. Today's lesson says that there is nothing inherent in anything that gives it a set value or meaning, and that no event, object, or person can determine your happiness. You alone define what is important to you and what is not.

When you are addicted to something or someone, it is because you have invested too much in one area, thinking it will bring happiness. You are compulsively pursuing something that continually leaves you feeling empty inside. A true statement about your life is:

> **Real choice, which leads to happiness and opportunity, comes from realizing that I give everything all the meaning it has for me.**

To understand today's lesson, visually scan your current environment. Start with things that are close to you, and apply today's lesson to everything you see around you, large or small, people or objects, bright or dull. Then broaden your gaze and look all around you, near and far, and apply the lesson to everything you see, hear, taste, smell, or feel. Do not try to systematically include everything. Instead, just relax and apply the lesson to anything that comes into your awareness. Do not decide to exclude anything either. Simply apply it equally to everything, regardless of your feelings of attachment or nonattachment to anyone or anything.

Repeat to yourself:

> I give this chair all the meaning it has for me.
> I give these clothes all the meaning that they have for me.
> I give this person all the meaning they have for me.
> I give this substance (drug, food, alcohol, and so on)
> all the meaning that it has for me.

Periodically throughout the day practice applying the lesson. If you catch yourself operating from the Addictive Personality, say:

> Peace comes from within me and is not determined by people, places, substances, or things.

✎ LESSON TWO

Preoccupying my mind with the past keeps me from discovering happiness and opportunity in the present.

When you allow yourself to become burdened by guilt and shame, you are operating in the Addictive Personality's belief that the past should always determine how you feel and react in the present. The Truth-Based Personality recognizes that:

> It is impossible to be consumed with guilt
> and have happiness at the same time.
>
> It is impossible to be consumed with shame
> and see new opportunities at the same time.
>
> When feelings of guilt, shame, low self-esteem,
> or negative self-judgment arise, I am not at peace.
>
> It is because I am looking upon everything
> and everyone through the distorting filter of the past.

Peace, happiness, and new opportunities
abide in the freedom of the present moment.

When you identify with the past you create blocks to experiencing the positive effects of the Truth-Based Personality. When you use the past as a source of knowledge so that you can pass judgment and induce guilt, you further isolate yourself from love.

Today, be determined to break the cycle of the Addictive Personality. Begin by sitting comfortably with your eyes closed. Observe your mind. Note each thought as it comes and goes. Try not to spend too much time on any one thought. Simply watch your thoughts for a few minutes, with as little attachment as possible to each thought. Identify each thought by naming the central figure or theme of it. For example, as your thoughts come and go, repeat to yourself:

I am now thinking about (central figure or theme).
And now I am thinking about (central figure or theme).

As you observe your thinking, note how many of your thoughts are based in the guilt-producing past. After a few minutes of this, say to yourself:

My mind is preoccupied with thoughts from the past.
But the past is gone, and today I am willing to let it go.

In the present moment I recognize my essential value
and look upon myself with forgiving eyes.

If I am in conflict, it is because my mind is preoccupied
with the past.
But the past is gone.

Therefore, I choose to see this (situation/person/object) only in the
peace of the present moment.

As simple as it sounds, observing your thoughts without becoming distracted by them can be difficult. But it is worth the effort, and with time this practice will bring you peace. It also serves as a foundation for many of the lessons that follow.

✍ LESSON THREE

I am not a victim. I can change my experience by changing my thoughts.

Your Addictive Personality confuses you by convincing you that you are a victim, that you are weak, but at the same time it deludes you into believing that you have the power to control your external circumstances. When you inevitably fail, your first reaction is to blame. The belief that strength is a denial of weakness is completely backward, but you are confused by the flimflam of the Addictive Personality.

Though you may be reluctant to admit it, you are probably a habitual finger-pointer. When you blame others, you believe you are a victim, give up your personal power, and relinquish the ability to create the life you want.

Some people get so used to being victims, they don't know what they want in life, but complain bitterly about not having it. Decide today not to be one of them. In order to recognize your strength, and to understand that you have choice, today focus upon a simple fact:

I am not a victim.
My own thoughts and beliefs
determine what I see and what I experience.
When I see the world as responsible for how I feel,
I am seeing myself as a victim,
and consistent peace is impossible.
However, regardless of the circumstances I find myself in,
I can maintain my power to choose the direction of my thoughts.
When I am stuck in a rut,
it may be because I am seeing myself as a victim.
Today, if I feel victimized, I will not attack another or defend myself.
Instead, I will remind myself:
I am not a victim of the world I see.
I choose the feelings I experience,
and I decide upon my own goals.
Changing my mind and seeing that I am not a victim is how
I become free to create new positive experiences and opportunities.

☙ Lesson Four

I can see all situations as opportunities to recognize essential value in myself and others.

You are constantly choosing between the Addictive Personality and the Truth-Based Personality. You are always only a choice away from peace. Today's lesson focuses on the fact that you have the ability to direct your mind.

Peace of mind and new opportunities begin in your own mind. When you are not peaceful, it is because your eyes are closed to recognizing essential value, which is love. When you see yourself as separate from others in a world that appears to be harsh, without meaning, threatening, and fragmented, you end up seeing yourself as vulnerable and in constant need of defense. But you can choose instead to see a united world where every situation offers you the opportunity to learn through recognizing the essential value in yourself and other people. If you become depressed, sad, hopeless, angry, guilty, or fearful, say to yourself:

I can choose peace *right now* instead of this.
I can create new opportunities *right now* from this challenge.
I do so by recognizing the essential value
in myself and other people.

If you find yourself caught in the Addictive Personality's cycle of judging yourself or others, repeat to yourself:

I want peace of mind and new opportunities.
Instead of judging, I choose to put my energy into recognizing
essential value and practicing forgiveness.

By concentrating on forgiveness you train your mind to know where to look for peace and opportunity, and how to create purpose and potential in every relationship. You come to understand that there is no need to wait any longer for peace of mind or effective communication, because forgiveness is a choice you can make each minute of every day.

To demonstrate and ensure my choice for peace,
and to discover new opportunity in every challenge,
I let all my actions stem from recognizing the essential value
in myself and others.

◠ LESSON FIVE

Let me recognize the real problem so it can be solved.

The Addictive Personality says that in order to solve your problems and be happy you need to change someone or some circumstance. It also tells you that acquiring something new can lessen your problem. The last thing the Addictive Personality would have you do is look at the contents of your thoughts, for this would reveal the flimsy foundation on which it is built. The Addictive Personality presents you with endless problems to be solved, yet always keeps the real problem hidden.

You cannot solve a problem if you do not know what it is. Today, instead of seeing yourself as having a number of problems to solve, concentrate on recognizing the one problem that is at the root of all others: the belief that you are unworthy of the life you want, separate from love, alone, and empty.

This belief is *the only* problem that needs to be addressed, because it is the feelings of emptiness and unworthiness that lead you to look outside of yourself for happiness.

Today, be determined to look at the real problem. Seeing the underlying consistency to all problems is the first step to realizing that you have the means to solve them.

Sit comfortably and close your eyes. Tell yourself, "My only problem is that I feel empty and unworthy, and so I look outside of myself for happiness." As you allow your mind to become quiet, invite the awareness of love to replace your list of worries. One by one, gently release each "problem" from your mind. As you let go, notice the tranquility that comes from ceasing to worry. Tell yourself:

> Whatever the problem, love is the answer.
> When problems arise, let me not be deceived
> about what the *real* problem is.
> Let me recognize that the *real* problem
> is my lack of an awareness of love.
> I invite love to make itself known to me.
> Whereas yesterday I saw endless problems,
> today I see boundless love.

✍ LESSON SIX

Forgiveness and compassion offer everything I want.

Your Addictive Personality tells you that constant analysis and judgment ensure your safety and bring you what you want. But these activities are born of fear and scarcity, and only perpetuate greater fear and more scarcity. Today, instead of judging, choose to practice the gentle means that heals the Addictive Personality: forgiveness and compassion.

True peace and happiness don't come from the transient satisfaction of getting what your Addictive Personality wants. Consistent peace of mind, true happiness, and endless opportunities are possible only through forgiveness and living a compassionate life. When you judge another person, when you decide they are guilty and undeserving of forgiveness, you reinforce your own sense of guilt and unworthiness. This is because what you see is your own repressed guilt projected outward.

Forgiveness is always the peaceful solution. Forgiveness that is based on unity recognizes that to free another from the chains of the past is to unbind yourself as well. In short, forgiveness is the water that extinguishes the raging fire of the Addictive Personality, and makes acting in compassionate ways possible.

Today, begin to use forgiveness and compassion as a means to bring about peace, healing, and happiness. Start by thinking of someone you dislike, find challenging, or see as having done something "unforgivable" to you. Close your eyes and picture this person standing in front of you. Tell yourself that remaining upset with this person is really hurting you, and that you want to free yourself. Remind yourself that holding onto a painful past does not help you now nor will it help you in the future. Look upon this person as if you know nothing of his or her "wrongdoing." Send a ray of compassion to this once fearful and hateful person. Allow your compassion to spread, permeating and surrounding this person, until your mental image is bright and unmarred by the past. Hold this image in your mind for a few minutes. Notice how peaceful you feel as you release the past and allow compassion to surround this person. After a few minutes, open your eyes and tell yourself:

Forgiveness and compassion offer everything I want.
As peace and happiness are my goals,
forgiveness and compassion are my path to these goals.

✍ LESSON SEVEN

All thoughts that I have toward other people are given to myself.

The Addictive Personality always separates, severing the connections between your thoughts, your health, your success, and your feelings about yourself. This is like denying the connection between the moon and the tides, or the sun and the growth of a flower. It is completely unnatural. You may not realize that your thinking determines your experience and influences your health and well-being, but your thoughts are like a boomerang, always coming back to you.

Today, embrace the idea that giver and receiver are the same, that what you put out you receive back. Imagine what life would be like today if you had no goal other than peace, if you saw no value in negative judgment, and in all situations were kinder than you need to be. You would be giving yourself the gift of peace of mind, health, and success.

In your communication with other people, if you offer acceptance, understanding, honesty, and forgiveness, you will find all the joy you are looking for. If you offer judgment, attack, fear, and condemnation, you will be inviting distance and suffering into your life. Examine your own past communications to see how this simple truth operates. Then start fresh today by saying to yourself:

> Today I want peace and so I will offer only this to others.
> Today I choose to hold kindness in my heart for others,
> and wish for them what I want for myself,
> even if I feel hurt by them.
> I do so not because I am superior or because I am inferior,
> but because opening the door to forgiveness is how I heal,
> and how I create a future for myself and others
> free of the limitations of past resentments and anger.

Again, remind yourself that all thoughts are like a boomerang, and vow today to choose accordingly. Now close your eyes and spend a few minutes thinking of people in your life while focusing on deepening your wish for healing and happiness for them.

If you have a lot of anger about something, this lesson will not come easy, but it is worth the effort. The goal is not to deny your upset, but to open the door to what is beyond it, and to see that staying upset and with-holding forgiveness ultimately hurts and limits yourself. Ask yourself,

Am I, *right now,* giving what I want for myself?

If not, simply direct your mind and begin giving to others what you want for yourself. In doing so you will discover the secret of creating what you want in life.

⮜ Lesson Eight

I will know what is of value and what is valueless.

Nothing, in itself, has value. You determine what you feel is valuable and what is not. When you assign so much value to something that it results in an external pursuit of happiness, you are operating in the Addictive Personality. This is important to remember, for you may behave as though you can't live without something, forgetting that you gave it all the value that is has for you. This is equally true of relationships.

What you value determines what you want. Love, for example, is eternal, and is therefore valuable. This is what has been termed in this book as *Essential Value.* Time can never diminish its worth. Yet it is important to realize that it is not the impermanent things in themselves that bring suffering, it is our *attachment* to them that creates suffering and conflict. To determine your level of attachment, ask yourself, if you lost [specify], how would it affect your peace of mind?

Once you realize that valuing the valuable ensures peace and valuing the valueless creates conflict, you are on the path to peace of mind. Yet what are the criteria for deeming something either valuable or valueless? Today's lesson addresses this question.

Will what I want last forever?
If not, it is valueless.
Will getting what I want result in someone else's loss?
If it will, it is valueless and will not bring me lasting happiness.
Remember, to give is to receive.
To receive at another's expense only harms myself.
Why is what I want of value to me?
Arms can be used to strike in anger or embrace in love.

An airplane can drop bombs or packages of food.
If I want happiness, healing, and abundance,
I will use all things as a means to create happiness and abundance.
Things are, in themselves, not bad,
my attachment to them, or misuse of them,
makes me a slave to them.

Whatever you value is what you think will bring happiness, yet pursuit of it may result in frustration, depression, loss, and despair. Use hard honesty today to determine if you have placed value on the valueless. Perhaps you think that things like money or prestige will give your life meaning. There is no problem in creating an abundant life, but when you look to certain things for happiness you are valuing the valueless and will always end up in a cycle of suffering. If you want a truly abundant life, begin today to know what is valuable and what is valueless.

∽ LESSON NINE

Today, I offer love instead of defensiveness.

When you operate from the Addictive Personality, you are busy building defensive walls watching out for potential losses and attacks. New opportunities are lost because you can't be open to the life you want when you remain behind a fortress of fear and repeat the same old patterns.

When you defend yourself, you mistakenly believe that your defenses, if they are strong enough, will protect you and bring you what you think you want. But these defenses only keep you isolated and afraid. In truth, your walls of defense lock out the new and different life you want, and repeat the cycle of suffering.

You are mistaken if you think that your defenses protect you. In fact, your defenses simply help perpetuate the cycle of attack and defense. Nobody builds defenses who does not have fear in his or her heart, and it is fear that blinds us to opportunity in life.

You make defenses because you fear attack. Yet with each new defense, your fear of attack increases. How can defenses offer safety when they escalate fear? Today, recognize the truth about your defenses:

Defenses always bring what they were meant to guard against.
Defensiveness sets up a cycle in which I cannot be at peace.

Attack leads to defense and defense leads to attack.
Today, instead of making my armor thicker,
I invite the power of love and compassion into my life.
Today, I replace my defenses with love,
which needs no defense.
Love grows when it is shared.
Love is unaffected by time.
Waiting for me, beneath my defenses,
is undisturbed peace and endless opportunities.
This peace and these opportunities I will find today.
If I defend myself I am attacked.
There is another way to be, which creates the outcome I long for.
Love is what I want and love needs no defense.

Today I offer love instead of defensiveness.

✏ LESSON TEN

The power of choice is always available to me.

Your ability to choose is what constitutes your freedom. The power to decide which thoughts to hold in your mind is the most powerful tool you have, for it makes you the director of your own life. You are always choosing between the Addictive Personality and the Truth-Based Personality. Each decision you make determines your experience. Today, make this process a conscious one, and by doing so realize the power of choice.

You decide what to believe and thus choose your experience. It is not the world that molds and shapes you; you do it yourself. If you are in conflict, it is because you have accepted a false belief as true.

You are the director of your life. You get to choose between a script containing only scenes of peace and a horror story with terror, loss, and attack lurking in every corner. Whether you realize it or not, you are always choosing, but your power of choice is a tool that you may have forgotten how to use to your benefit. Today, learn that your power of choice can ensure your peace of mind.

The power of choice is my own.
Today, I use this power to choose only love-based thoughts.

There is a quiet place within you that is undisturbed, full of love, and complete. When you quiet your mind and direct your thoughts you can always choose to enter this place. As a reminder of the choice you wish to make today, review the summary of the Core Beliefs of the Truth-Based Personality on page 101 and the summary of the Alternate Messages of the Truth-Based Personality on page 129. Today, if you find yourself in conflict, repeat to yourself:

Right now my power of choice can change my experience.
I can choose to direct my mind to the Truth-Based Personality
instead of the confusing chatter of the Addictive Personality.

⤳ LESSON ELEVEN

Today I learn that giving and receiving are one.

When you are stuck in the Addictive Personality, you believe that the more you get, take, buy, and conquer, the happier and more secure you will feel. Your emphasis is always on getting, never on giving. When you do give, it is usually in the interests of manipulation, a way to get something that you want. By contrast, the Truth-Based Personality says that to give is to receive.

The way you see others is the way you see yourself. If you see others as having done unforgivable things, so must you see yourself. If you look upon one person or one thousand with condemnation and hate, so you must condemn and hate yourself. Likewise, when you see others through the soft, loving eyes of forgiveness, you will love and forgive yourself.

Today, you can learn there is no lapse of time between giving and receiving. As you give, so do you receive. This is why peace is always a possible alternative. Today's lesson offers the alternative to insecurity, loneliness, and loss because:

You can give and receive forgiveness and compassion
at any moment you choose.

Today's lesson is very practical. You can practice it easily and continually throughout the day. As you see the results and verify the benefits for yourself, the truth of giving and receiving will become clear to you.

Today, I offer understanding, kindness, and compassion

to everyone I meet or think about.
Today, I will see how quickly the awareness of my own
essential value returns to me.
To give is to receive. I will receive what I am giving now.

Then, picture in your mind a specific person and say, for example:

To this person I offer peace of mind.
To this person I offer tranquility.
To this person I offer calmness.

Again, try not to exclude anyone today from the gifts you give, because, in the end, any exclusion is an exclusion of yourself. Every person you meet today offers you another opportunity to learn that giving and receiving are one, and that peace is possible. If you find yourself hostile or defensive, ask yourself:

Is this what I want to give myself?

✎ LESSON TWELVE

I direct my mind, which I alone am responsible for.

Today, you can begin to tame your unruly mind by realizing that you determine the thoughts that you think and thus the experiences that you have.

Take the first step by deciding to take responsibility for your own feelings and thoughts. Today, understand that you alone direct your mind, choosing between the Addictive Personality and the Truth-Based Personality. You alone decide which thoughts to have, what purpose your life holds, and how to act. Today, determine to direct your own mind, for which you alone are responsible.

Most people put the cart before the horse; they think that purpose, happiness, and abundance come from focusing on the world around them, rather than their own mind. If you are to have a happy, purposeful, and abundant life, you must first take charge of your thoughts. Today, see that you can always direct your mind to recognize and align with the Truth-Based Personality. Whenever you experience an unwanted thought, you can silently say,

"If I am to have a happy, purposeful, and abundant life, I must first take charge of my own mind."

I direct my mind, which I alone am responsible for.
I choose to let go of this belief
of the Addictive Personality (specify),
and direct my mind toward this belief
of the Truth-Based Personality (specify).
This is how I find happiness and create new opportunity.

✎ LESSON THIRTEEN

Today I will stop judging everything that occurs.

Judging others and yourself increases fear and guilt, shutting the door on opportunity and healing. Begin today by asking yourself the following questions:

If I stopped judging for one day, what would that day be like?
If I chose to concentrate on extending compassion instead of
judgment, how would my experience change?
If I devoted a day to practicing Recognizing Essential Value rather
than passing judgment, how would I feel around other people and
how would my relationships unfold?

The thoughts you hold toward others affect how you feel about yourself. For example, you cannot simultaneously feel hatred toward somebody and feel love for yourself. It would be like trying to exhale and inhale in the same moment. You may have previously learned that it is both natural and healthy to judge situations and people, that it enables you to make good decisions. Today, begin to retrain your mind to see that your negative judgments and past resentments do nothing but create feelings of anger and separateness. The Truth-Based Personality recognizes that any thought or action that condemns results in fear, guilt, and aloneness, and thus limits your opportunities in life.

Today, I leave life and love
free to exist undisturbed by my judgments.
Instead of judgment and separation,
I look at the interdependency of all life,
of which I am an integral part.
Today, I will view all people and events without negative judgment.

If I am tempted to pass judgment, I will remind myself that
if I judge this person
I will rob myself of growth and opportunity.
Today, I turn away from my old habit
of judgment and condemnation.
In looking for guidance, I turn my focus inward,
toward my heart.
Today, I trade the sword of judgment
for a tender thought of compassion,
and peace dawns in my mind.

๛ LESSON FOURTEEN

Today I stop seeing myself as limited.

The Addictive Personality promotes limitation in every way possible, but never lets you recognize it. It tells you to feel empty and that you can be filled only by someone or something outside yourself, such as a substance, a possession, or a relationship. Today, devote yourself to seeing that you are whole with unlimited potential. Only your beliefs limit your happiness and stifle your potential for opportunity. The only limits you have are self-imposed.

All thoughts of limitations are restrictive to relationships. When you place limits on others, you bind yourself as well. There is no greater gift you can give than letting go of limitations. By doing so you unshackle yourself and those around you. Every limit that you impose on yourself or others is a chain that inhibits your growth. Today, give yourself strength by seeing the power of love everywhere and in everything.

Limitations, which are created by the Addictive Personality, seem very real. But regardless of the limitation, the solution is the same: remember that you lack nothing to experience love and compassion this instant.

Today, begin to challenge any limitation, no matter how real it seems. For example, inadequate time and money are common inventions of the Addictive Personality. You may think that you do not have enough time to pause to relax, or perhaps not enough money to be happy and secure. But remember, even when you impose a limitation on yourself, you can always challenge it. For example, if you feel you lack time or money, you might use a positive affirmation to change the negative feeling.

I am limitless.
Do I not have the time to send a kind thought?
Can I not afford to extend compassion from my heart?

The specific words are not important as long as you question the validity of every limit you have imposed, or are tempted to set. Especially question any phrase that can complete the following sentence: "Peace of mind is not possible now because _____." The most important thing you can do today is to remind yourself hourly:

I am not limited in my ability to be happy and prosperous.
You are not limited in your ability to be happy and prosperous.
We are not limited in our ability to be happy and prosperous.

✍ LESSON FIFTEEN

This day I choose to have peace of mind as my single goal.

The Addictive Personality says that the only way to find peace would be to have all of your emotional needs met by another person, all the material possessions you ever wanted, a perfect body, and the ability to control all situations. The problem is that your list of needs is endless, your desire to control is compulsive, the perfect body is elusive, and peace is impossible.

Today, understand that this is not the way to peace. Peace has never left your mind; it is you who have left it. But you can return to it by having faith that peace is within you now; it is only covered by a thin veil of addictive thoughts. Today, look past this veil and rest in the quiet peace that awaits you. Today's lesson is a declaration that inner peace is possible if you just give it a chance to emerge. Instead of listening to the confusion of your Addictive Personality, make peace of mind your single goal.

It may not seem possible to spend an entire day, or even an hour, in peace. Perhaps you think that if you were in a more ideal situation, then you would find peace. This "if-only . . ." thought system leads nowhere but to more suffering. Reverse this thought system by telling yourself many times throughout the day:

Right now I have everything I need to have peace of mind.
If peace of mind is my single goal today,
what would I do now to ensure it?

I can reach out to heal a relationship that has been wounded.
I can let go of an ancient grudge.
I can focus on giving instead of receiving.
I can extend thoughts of compassion when normally I would
defend myself or judge someone else.
I can do something nurturing for myself.

Now make your own list, with specifics, and commit yourself to carrying it out.

⚮ LESSON SIXTEEN

I will not invest in fear today.

With any kind of investment, your yield depends on whether it is sound or flimsy. The Addictive Personality leads you down a path that results in poor investments, where you ultimately end up too afraid to see the truth about yourself. A mind that is full of guilt, fear, and judgment cannot see its owner's essential value. Guilt is a product of your past and is invested in maintaining your feelings of unworthiness. Today, rather than continuing to invest your energy in this cycle of fear, choose to welcome that which can heal your misconceptions about yourself: choose to invest in love.

The foundation of your belief system is simple: you identify with and invest in what you think will make you safe and bring you prosperity. When you choose the Addictive Personality, you believe that judgment, defenses, and attack are the keys to safety and prosperity, and so you invest your time and energy in fear. When you choose the Truth-Based Personality you believe that safety and prosperity lie in acceptance, forgiveness, and compassion, and so you invest your time and energy in love. What you choose to invest in, fear or love, will determine your feelings about yourself, what you experience, your level of abundance, and your outlook on the world. We get to choose what to invest in each and every moment of our lives.

Today, invite truth into your mind by investing wisely. You have grown tired of the illusions and flimflam of the Addictive Personality, which is why you are reading this book. Love is your safety, so invest in it with confidence. Once you invest wholeheartedly in your true self, you need not worry about fear, for fear cannot exist where love is present.

When you invest your energy in developing the Truth-Based Personality you will feel safe, and you will see prosperity come into your life. When you invest in the Addictive Personality you invest in fear, and as a result you limit opportunity and constantly run to or from someone or something. Today, invest wisely. Remind yourself hourly:

> I invest in the truth of who I am and I am safe.
> I invest in love and I yield all that is of value.
> I invest in love and I discover new opportunity.

Today, see the truth about fear by recognizing its presence in your life. When fear arises, face it, and stop investing your valuable energy in it. As you do, you will find that fear does not exist separately from the mind that made it.

> The Addictive Personality stops the moment I stop investing in it.
> Fear stops the moment I stop making it and
> believing in my creation.
> Fear, in and of itself, does not exist;
> it is formed and fueled by my investment in it.
> When I find myself fearful, I remember that
> I have invested unwisely.
> Only my mind can produce fear,
> and my mind can also stop fear.
> Fear is overcome when I stop and invest in love instead.
> I welcome what my sound investments bring today.

☙ Lesson Seventeen

Nothing except my thoughts can hurt me. Nothing except my thoughts can heal me.

Realizing the truth of this simple statement is the first step toward freedom. It is the prescription for healing the Addictive Personality. In the past, when you have been hurt, you may have looked to others as the cause of your suffering. Or perhaps you blamed your unhappiness on bad luck or unfortunate situations. Today, reverse this way of thinking by realizing that you can be hurt or healed by nothing but your own thoughts.

When you find yourself suffering in any way, it is helpful to examine your thoughts. This will help begin to heal the only thing that can hurt you in any way: your own mind. Many times throughout the day, especially if you are facing a particular challenge, read the following whenever you have a few free moments:

> Because my thoughts can either free me or imprison me,
> it is with my thoughts that I must work.
> I can change my thoughts about the world, about others,
> and about myself.
> I cannot change other people or many of the situations
> in which I find myself,
> but I can learn from them.

When you are hurt it is because you have accepted one or more of the core beliefs of the Addictive Personality as true. Despite your habit of blaming your pain on other people and situations, this is *the only* reason you are ever hurt. You are always, every second of the day, choosing the thoughts that fill your mind and thus are choosing your experience and the actions you will take. When you focus your attention on your thoughts, you can learn to choose the contents of your thoughts, and, in turn, what you experience in life. If you are not aware of your thoughts you will continue to feel that you have no choice about what you experience.

Stop letting the Addictive Personality rule your mind. Today, consciously choose which thoughts to hold in your mind. In this way you can direct your mind away from hurt and toward new opportunities. Begin to direct your mind by practicing the following:

1. Whenever you find yourself feeling in any way other than peaceful, identify the core belief of the Addictive Personality that you are holding in your mind.

2. Tell yourself that it is this thought that is causing your suffering.

3. Turn inward and say to yourself,

> This belief is false and doesn't reflect who I am.
> It is bringing hurt, not healing, to my life.

I can elect to change this addictive thought.

✐ Lesson Eighteen

Let me remember why I am here.

If you were always aware of why you are here and what every situation is really for, you would always know your true purpose: experiencing love by practicing forgiveness and extending compassion. Knowing your purpose, there would be no reason to listen to the irrationality of the Addictive Personality. It is in remembering why you are here that opportunity and healing can come into your life. Today, concentrate on remembering why you are here.

When you forget that your goal is peace of mind, you become confused and conflicted, unsure of your direction, and, ultimately, unsure of who you are and why you are here. When you forget your purpose, you become like a robot that automatically responds to external circumstances. When you forget why you are here, you judge others. In the absence of the awareness of the Truth-Based Personality you think your purpose for being here is to receive instead of give, and to condemn instead of accept. You become obsessively involved in pursuing conflicting goals, which never lead to happiness or realized opportunity because they have no value.

When I have conflicting goals, conflict is all I will achieve.

Conflicting goals make you depressed, frustrated, fearful, and angry. You can escape from conflicting goals by identifying which goal is bringing you suffering. Release that goal and keep the one you know will bring you what you truly want. The key to remembering why you are here is to discipline your mind to identify and let go of what does not lead to healing, happiness, and opportunity. An unexamined mind goes unchanged.

You can escape the suffering caused by conflicting goals by choosing to remember why you are here. You can tell yourself, especially in challenging circumstances:

I am here to learn the methods and means of love.

This situation (specify) is occurring to help teach me
what I am here to learn.

➷ LESSON NINETEEN

Today all I see is opportunity for happiness, healing, and abundance.

When you look at yourself through the window of the past, it is like looking in a curved amusement park mirror: you see a distorted image of yourself. Today, with each new breath, move into a new moment, untouched by the past. Today your goal is to embrace your happiness through consciously living in this new moment. The only thing that you need to do to experience your happiness is to change your mind from being focused on the past to being focused on the present. The present moment is a beautifully wrapped gift of healing. It is waiting for you to open it.

Only when you look at a distorted past and anticipate a fearsome future does your present happiness escape you. When you see a world full of separation, what you see is painful and frightening. Do not allow yourself to be deceived into thinking that guilt is inescapable, because in the present moment guilt does not exist. Guilt is always the by-product of the past; happiness and opportunity are the results of the present moment. Today, begin to see that there is no value in holding onto the past.

Throughout this day, seek to find nothing but your present happiness, and look upon only what you seek. Do not obsessively wish that something could be different, and don't invite fear into your mind by thinking that the future will duplicate the past. Don't waste this precious moment on irrationally wishing for a better past. Realize that the only thing that keeps you from experiencing peace of mind is your procrastination in accepting it, for peace of mind is always available to you in the present moment. Further, instead of focusing on getting something, focus on letting all that is good emerge naturally from the moment. Today is about letting, not getting, so repeat to yourself often:

The past is past.
The future is in the future.
Today all I see is opportunity
for happiness, healing, and abundance.

❧ LESSON TWENTY

This moment is all there is; being kind is what this moment is for.

Today's lesson is an extension of yesterday's in that the emphasis is on living in the present moment and knowing what it is for. When your mind is focused on kindness, the present moment expands and becomes all that exists in your awareness. Fear diminishes as you consciously hold kind thoughts in your mind.

If you want a tranquil mind you must change your idea about the purpose of time. You may have seen time as both a judge and a prison guard, sentencing you to the guilt of the past and the worry of the future, overlooking the serenity of the present moment. Such a concept of time defeats your goal of healing and inner peace and hides kindness from your awareness. How you perceive time determines what you will experience.

Emphasis upon the past produces guilt.
Emphasis upon the future produces worry and fear.
Emphasis upon the present yields kindness.

You may mistakenly have thought that kindness was something to be earned or achieved. You may have thought that you had to do something to deserve a kind thought or action. The experience of true kindness is a result of recognizing essential value in yourself and others, and this always takes place in the present moment. Kindness is not earned or achieved, it is remembered in the present moment, where it awaits patiently. You may have thought that you had to wait for certain things to be accomplished or changed in order to deserve kindness or to offer it; the only thing that needs to change is your belief about time.

When I am anything less than joyous,
when I feel a lack of any kind,
when I want something I don't have,
when I think that peace is impossible
because of what has happened
or that peace is impossible
because of what has not happened,
all I need is but to remind myself
to change my mind about time.
This moment is all there is; being kind is what this moment is for.

⌒ LESSON TWENTY-ONE

Fear imprisons me; forgiveness sets me free.

Today's lesson idea is a summary: The Addictive Personality is full of fear, judgment, and guilt that bind you in conflict, external pursuits for happiness, and endless suffering. The Truth-Based Personality is full of compassion, caring, forgiveness, and peace that heals your mind, cleanses your perception, and brings you true happiness and endless opportunity.

I once heard a joke told about an old man with a long beard and tattered clothes who sat in a prison cell. His jailor said, "Well, I have good news and bad news. The good news is that the cell door is unlocked. The bad news is that it has been that way for the last twenty-five years."

The cell door, created by your Addictive Personality, which has kept you imprisoned from happiness and opportunity for so long, has never been locked. You can choose to leave your cell at any time simply by realizing this. When you realize how alike everyone is in their yearning for kindness, understanding, and compassion, it will become much harder to judge them and yourself. Today, allow the darkness of the Addictive Personality to be healed by the light of forgiveness. No longer can separation, fear, and conflict be called by other names, or denied, or projected onto someone or something else, avoided, hidden, or disguised.

The obstacles to forgiveness, and, therefore, to happiness and opportunity, arise when you accept the Addictive Personality's fearful beliefs as true. As you gently remove these obstacles, the awareness of happiness and opportunity becomes free to blossom and grow.

Choose to no longer hold yourself and the world in fear. Today, use no relationship, object, or situation to keep yourself mired in the past. Instead, in all situations, and with everyone you meet, see that another opportunity for peace and healing is given to you.

With every new moment, you can ensure your peace of mind by practicing forgiveness before it passes. Toward each person you see or think about, offer a gentle thought of forgiveness, and accept the same for yourself.

Fear imprisons me.

Forgiveness sets me free.

This is the key to my healing.

AN ELEVEN-WEEK ACTION PLAN FOR CONTINUED HEALING

Although I have tried to make the concepts in this book as simple, direct, and practical as possible, I have used a few new terms and I have used some terms in a slightly different manner than you may have previously encountered. The following will serve to keep a focus on healing and to help you continue applying the new ideas presented in this book to your daily life. I suggest you practice each for one week, and keep a daily journal of your experiences. Whereas the twenty-one daily lessons you practiced are quite specific, these weeks are more general. As you practice, you may wish to return to the parts of the book that coincide with the topic.

1. **Recognizing the Addictive Personality:** This week I devote to becoming aware of any thoughts based upon fear, judgment, and separation, that result in suffering through an external pursuit for happiness.

2. **Developing the Truth-Based Personality:** This week I devote to developing a thought system based upon love, forgiveness, and commonality, that results in peace of mind, healing, and new opportunities.

3. **Understanding Recognized Essential Value (REV):** This week I devote to developing a mindful practice of seeing beyond shame, guilt, negative behavior, and fear where the true value of every person is recognized.

4. **Recognizing Being Compulsively-Other-Focused (COF):** This week I devote to becoming aware of when my emotional needs are not being met, how I may rely on a maladaptive learned behavior that stems from my belief that happiness and security come from controlling, or being needed by, other people.

5. **Recognizing Projection:** This week I devote to becoming aware of how I unconsciously project my guilt and low self-worth away from myself and onto someone else. If I am angry or upset, I look at this process to see a way out.

6. **Practicing Extension:** In contrast to projection, this week I devote to developing a practice of the Truth-Based Personality based upon the true belief that as I give what is truly valuable, I receive that which I give.

7. **Recognizing Denial:** This week I devote to becoming aware of the unconscious defense mechanism of the Addictive Personality that keeps my painful realities, memories, and feelings hidden because of the belief they would overpower me. I see how this process also disowns the truth of who I am, which is love.

8. **Practicing Hard Honesty:** This week I devote to becoming persistent and penetrating in looking at my thinking, actions, and lifestyle. I develop a practice of recognizing, observing, and evaluating the beliefs that make up and rule the Addictive Personality.

9. **Understanding the Power Over Approach:** This week I devote to becoming aware of how I use, or have used, pride, blind willpower, manipulation, condemnation, and control.

10. **Practicing the Powerlessness Approach:** This week I devote to developing humility, intention, acceptance, and honesty.

11. **Practicing Peaceful Persistence:** This week I devote to the practice of standing up for myself and truth while maintaining peace of mind. This is done by directing my mind to pay attention to my thoughts and attitudes rather than avoiding, blaming, complaining, judging, finding fault, and being afraid. Think "Buddhist squeaky wheel."

EPILOGUE

At one time in my life I felt that my heart was dying a slow death, that I had no choice but to slip deeper into the hopeless despair of fear and addiction. It is no small miracle that through practicing the principles in this book I can say to you that I now feel alive and grateful, and I welcome new opportunities each and every day. Most of the time I feel open, unguarded, and able to extend love. Today, I know there is not one being on this planet from whom I would withhold love, kindness, or compassion. I know that to give is to receive, and, for me, to not forgive is a form of slow suicide. Thank you for reading this book, for I teach what it is I most want to learn. In writing I continue to learn of the methods and means of love.

Peace to you and may your path be blessed.

UNFOLDING

Love always surrounds us in gentility,
yet we so often turn our backs,
walking aimlessly into darkness.

May we cease this futile pattern
and surrender to the serenity of love,
breathe in the joy of life.
Let us pass our days smiling upon each other
while extending our hands in kindness and forgiveness.
May we speak from the center of our being,
and allow others to know our hearts.
May we each feel the limitless depth
of love that abides in and around us,
and know that this is who we are.

INDEX

Repression of emotions, 123–124
Responsibility
    forgiveness and, 117
    freedom and opportunity from, 109
    taking, 95–96

S
Safety and defenselessness, 86–87
Scarcity, use of, 43–44
Searching, problem with, 97–98
Secrets, 63
Security and judgment, 47–48
Self-affirmation, 135–136
Self-blame, 41
Self-Confidence, Fearless, 97
Self-esteem
    from within, 98
    approval and, 120
    competence and, 120–121
    of compulsively-other-focused, 130–131
    judgment and, 40
    people pleasing, 54–55
    unconditional love and, 88–89
Self-fulfilling prophecy, 36–37
Self-improvement, 71
Self-talk, negative, 34, 65–66
Separateness, belief in, 45–47
Serenity, 30
Sexuality, 72
    homosexual experiences, 72
    intimacy and, 103
Shame, 15
    love and, 62
    Recognized Essential Value and, 72–73
    in special hate/love relationships, 26–28
Situations, 65
Smile for No Good Reason (Jampolsky), 90–91
Speaking, fear of, 51–52
Special hate/love relationships, 26–28
Stopping Addictive Personality behaviors, 98
Stress, feelings of, 121
Stuffing process, 90–91
Success, 97
    competition and, 53
    judgment and, 47–48

Suffering. See Pain
Surface change, 75–76

T
Team, creation of, 68
Teresa, Mother, 83
Thoughts
    changing, 93
    identifying irrational thoughts, 34
    irrational thoughts, 34
    lesson on, 151, 161–162
    system, 29–44
Time limitations, 127
Traps, patterns creating, 140
Trust, 87
    vs. trust, 118
Truth-Based Personality, 37–38, 59–84
    core beliefs, 85–102
    new patterns for, 69
Truth-based relationships, 138–139

U
Unconditional love, 88–89
Understanding and communication, 58
Unfolding, 169
Unity to life, 85–86

V
Value
    creating, 82–83
    lesson on, 152–153
    in truth-based relationships, 139
Victim role, lesson on, 147
Vulnerability, 28

W
Weakness, feelings of, 124
Website of author, 142
Wholeness, denial of, 23
Wisdom
    daily words of, 142
    judgment and, 41
Woods, Tiger, 67
Worldviews, 126
Worrying, 121
    pattern of, 92
    seeing beyond, 68

About the Author

Dr. Lee Jampolsky has served on the medical staffs and faculties of respected graduate schools and hospitals in Northern California. His numerous television appearances, radio broadcasts, and print interviews include *The Wall Street Journal, Business Week, Los Angeles Times,* and *Women's World.* He is the author of seven books, which have been translated into a dozen languages. Dr. Jampolsky is a sought-after international speaker whose approaches to creating a positive attitude for optimal performance, eliminating stress, practical spirituality, overcoming health challenges, and healing from addictions have transformed thousands of lives all over the world. For free daily Words of Wisdom, or for more information, please visit his website at www.DrLeeJampolsky.com.

Other Books Available from Celestial Arts